God selected th
His Tabernacle! God, being the Great Interior
Decorator of the universe, chose colors which would be
perfect for the Holy of Holies' sacred room: Purple,
Scarlet, and Blue.

There are three members of the Trinity and
interestingly, there are three colors that God selected
for the Holy of Holies. All three colors are "very
strong, dominant colors"! (There will be no pink or
gray or mauve in the Holy of Holies.)

'What if' each color represented one member of the
Trinity? It is only a guess but I suspect that Royal
Purple would probably represent the Father. Scarlet
would clearly portray Jesus who shed his blood for us.

The Blue remains, then, to be the Holy Spirit's color. In
Genesis, the Holy Spirit hovered over the earth just as
now blue sky covers the earth in a similar fashion. Blue
would be a wonderful expression of the Holy Spirit.

Mysteriously purple includes both blue and scarlet as
though the Father and Son and Holy Spirit are "One
Essence" but yet three individual members or colors.
Just as God is "Three in one" for the Trinity, in like
manner, royal purple is "three in one" for purple
contains both scarlet and blue.

A fourth color was also present in the Holy of Holies for decoration; that of pure gold clasps to hold the curtains. The book cover using purple, scarlet, blue and gold is a visual of the Holy of Holies' colors.

"Every skilled woman spun with her hands and brought what she had spun—blue, purple or scarlet yarn or fine linen." (Exodus 35: 25)

"All the skilled men among the workmen made the tabernacle with ten curtains of finely twisted linen and blue, purple and scarlet yarn, with cherubim worked into them by a skilled craftsman. All the curtains were the same size—twenty eight cubits (42 feet) long and four cubits (6 feet) wide... Then they made fifty gold clasps and used them to fasten the two sets of curtains together so that the tabernacle was a unit." (Exodus 36:8,9,13)

"In the beginning God created the heavens and the earth... and the Spirit of God was hovering over the waters." (Genesis 1:1, 2)

"Anyone who has seen me (Jesus) has seen the Father. How can you say, 'Show us the Father'? Don't you believe that I am in the Father, and that the Father is in me? The words I say to you are not just my own. Rather, it is the Father, living in me, who is doing his work. Believe me when I say that I am in the Father and the Father is in me…" (John 14:9-11)

"Now the Lord is the Spirit, and where the Spirit of the Lord is, there is freedom." (2 Corinthians 3:17)

What if the mystery of the Trinity is beyond our comprehension just like this triangle?

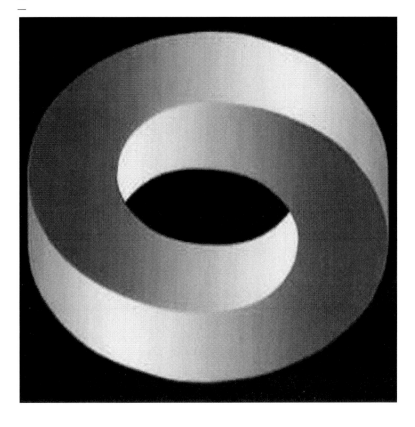

What if the mystery of eternity is beyond our comprehension just like this ring?

DEDICATION

To
Sandy Kaye Rupp
who has lovingly
been by my side
for 43 years!

What If?

A DEVOTIONAL OF POSSIBILITIES!

HENRY JACOB RUPP MD

TABLE OF CONTENTS

There is nothing quite as exciting as the "What Ifs" in life!

"What if" I had attended a different college or chosen a different occupation? "What if" Dad hadn't married Mom? I would only be half here! My whole life would have been changed drastically.

The "What Ifs" in life deal with "possibilities." Sometimes the "What If" possibilities thrill us or make us laugh. Other "What Ifs" speak deeply to us and challenge us to change. There are some "What Ifs" that we hope won't ever happen.

As your read each "What If" devotional, may you be challenged to live each day to the fullest in preparation for it becoming true! Read only one "What If" each day. They are meant to be savored and discussed with a friend.

"Can you fathom the mysteries of God? Can you probe the limits of the Almighty? They are higher than the heavens—what can you do? They are deeper than the depths of the grave —what can you know? Their measure is longer than the earth and wider than the sea. (Job 11:7-9)

"Great is the LORD and most worthy of praise; his greatness no one can fathom." (Psalm 145:3)

As you do not know the path of the wind, or how the body is formed in a mother's womb, so you cannot understand the work of God, the Maker of all things. (Ecclesiastes 11:5)

"Now we see but a poor reflection as in a mirror; then we shall see face to face. Now I know in part; then I shall know fully, even as I am fully known." (1 Corinthians 13:12)

What if God, who is love, decided to make an awesome supernatural display of love greater than any other display in creation?

What might God do to show awesome, amazing love to us? Consider these steps:

1. Create a beautiful creation.
2. Create humans to see the beautiful creation that was made specifically for them to enjoy.
3. Shower humans with love by giving each person amazing gifts:
   A. A billion dollar body containing a spiritual life (soul) made in the image of God.
   B. A free guiding service throughout life with a 'live-in' counselor.
   C. Love, joy peace, patience, kindness, goodness, gentleness, faithfulness, and self control along with many other special benefits.
   D. A Supernatural Book with specific directions on how to become prosperous and successful.
4. Display awesome supernatural love to the very people who inflicted Him with

incredible pain. (Author's note: Showing love out of excess is good; showing love out of sacrifice demonstrates even greater love; showing indescribable love to those who caused the deep personal pain demonstrates the most amazing, powerful love imaginable!)

Jesus Christ set aside His mighty power and glory in Heaven, then came down as God/Man and died for each one of us in the most unusual, supernatural display of love in all of creation! Nothing anywhere compares with God's display of incredible love.

"In the beginning God created the heavens and the earth". (Genesis 1:1)

"So God created man in his own image; in the image of God he created him; male and female he created them." (Genesis 1:27

"The Lord will guide you always…" (Isaiah 58:11)

"Don't you know that you yourselves are God's temple and that God's Spirit lives in you." (1 Corinthians 3:16)

"But the fruit of the Spirit is love, joy, peace, patience, kindness, goodness, faithfulness, gentleness and self-control." (Galatians 5:22)

"Do not let the Book of the Law (Bible) depart from your mouth; meditate on it day and night, so that you may be careful to do everything written in it. Then you will be prosperous and successful." (Joshua 1:8)

"Who, being in the very nature God, did not consider equality with God something to be grasped, but made himself nothing, taking the very nature of a servant, being made in human likeness. And being found in appearance as a man, he humbled himself and became obedient to death-even death on the cross!" (Philippians 2:6-8)

"Let us fix our eyes on Jesus, the author and perfecter of our faith, who for the joy set before him endured the cross, scorning its shame, and sat down at the right hand of the throne of God. Consider him who endured such opposition from sinful men, so that you will not grow weary and lose heart." (Hebrews 12:2, 3)

"Greater love has no one than this,that one lay down his life for his friends." (John 15:13)

"God so loved the world that He gave His only Son that whosoever believes in Him shall not perish but have everlasting life." (John 3:16)

What if God's beauty surpasses all other beauty in creation?

We rarely talk about God's awesome beauty. When we get to Heaven we will be thrilled as God displays new revelations of Himself. Nothing can be more beautiful than God who created beauty in the first place.

It is not wrong to imagine God's beauty! God the Father, God the Son, and God the Holy Spirit will express their individual beauty in unique ways which are perfectly contrasting and yet, perfectly compatible. Together, the Triune God will display absolute beauty unified as one.

In Heaven, we will experience God in ever increasing revelations! That will be the most awesome experience for all of eternity. God's awesome splendor will result in our ever increasing desire to worship and praise God forever.

The beauty of creation is just a small reflection of our Creator's beauty. Nothing in all creation can possibly compare with God's beauty! Anticipate God's awesome beauty which, for now, is beyond our imagination and comprehension!

"One thing I ask of the LORD, this is what I seek: that I may dwell in the house of the LORD all the days of my life, to gaze upon the beauty of the LORD and to seek him in his temple." (Psalm 27:4)

"Your eyes will see the king in his beauty and view a land that stretches afar." (Isaiah 33:17)

"Ascribe to the Lord the glory due his name; worship the Lord in the splendor of his holiness." (Psalm 29:2)

"O Lord my God, you are very great; you are clothed with splendor and majesty. He wraps himself in light as with a garment. . ." (Psalm 104:1)

"In that day the Branch of the LORD will be beautiful and glorious, and the fruit of the land will be the pride and glory of the survivors in Israel." (Isaiah 4:2)

What if I died, went to heaven, and Jesus Christ met me there and revealed something that shocked me?

He revealed that I had markedly underutilized the prayer power that He had set aside for me to use during my life on earth! Christ had wished for me to pray much more so that He could have answered far more prayer requests in wonderful miraculous ways.

What if I had used up only one percent of the prayer power that He intended for me to use while I was living on earth? It became clear to me that much of my weakness and discouragement on earth was because I had not earnestly prayed to unleash God's power that He had intended for me to use! Many times I didn't receive His powerful prayer answers because I had not even asked Him to help!

To underutilize God's prayer power is living like the poor person who doesn't know about the million dollars stashed under his sleeping mat that he could use. Don't underestimate the prayer power potential that God has available for you to use! God desires to unleash incredible power through your prayers.

What percentage of God's prayer power are you using? Is it 1 percent, 10 percent or perhaps none?

"Until now you have not asked for anything in my name. Ask and you will receive, and your joy will be complete." (John 16:24)

"And I will do whatever you ask in my name, so that the Son may bring glory to the Father. You may ask me for anything in my name, and I will do it." (John 14:13, 14)

"Ask and it will be given to you; seek and you will find; knock and the door will be opened to you. For everyone who asks receives; he who seeks finds; and to him who knocks, the door will be opened. Which of you, if his son asks for bread, will give him a stone? Or if he asks for a fish, will give him a snake? If you, then, though you are evil, know how to give good gifts to your children, how much more will your Father in heaven give good gifts to those who ask him!" (Matthew 7:7-11)

"Again, I tell you that if two of you on earth agree about anything you ask for, it will be done for you by my Father in heaven." (Matthew 18:19)

What if all of creation could easily be held in Jesus' hand like a baseball being held in the hand of a pitcher?

God initially breathed all of creation into existence out of nothing. There is estimated to be 10 to the 50th tons of matter in the universe. Scientists calculate that there are at least 100 billion galaxies each with 100 billion stars and innumerable planets including earth out there. All are in God's amazing control.

Some mistakenly feel that earth is getting out of God's control and that our individual problems are too many and too difficult for God to fix. When dealing with the immensity of our personal problems, reflect on God's power to create everything out of nothing and hold it all perfectly together! He is awesome in power and wisdom.

"In the beginning God created the heavens and the earth."(Genesis 1:1)

"For by Him all things were created; things in heaven and on earth, visible and invisible, whether thrones or powers or rulers or authorities; all things were created by him and for him. He is before all things. And in him all things hold together." (Colossians 1:16, 17)

"He determines the number of the stars and calls them each by name. Great is our Lord and mighty in power; his understanding has no limit." (Psalm 147:4, 5)

"But God made the earth by his power; he founded the world by his wisdom and stretched out the heavens by his understanding." (Jeremiah 10:15)

"He has made everything beautiful in its time. He has also set eternity in the hearts of men; yet they cannot fathom what God has done from beginning to end." (Ecclesiastes 3:11)

"Great is the LORD and most worthy of praise; his greatness no one can fathom... They will tell of the power of your awesome works, and I will proclaim your great deeds." (Psalm 145:3, 6)

"Do not be terrified by them, for the LORD your God, who is among you, is a great and awesome God." (Deuteronomy 7:21)

"Be strong and courageous. Do not be terrified;

do not be discouraged, for the Lord your God

will be with you wherever you go." (Joshua 1:9)

"Are not two sparrows sold for a penny? Yet not one
of them will fall to the ground apart from the will of
your Father. And even the very hairs of your head
are all numbered. So don't be afraid; you are worth
more than many sparrows." (Matthew 5:29, 30)

What if you are an astronaut and while you are outside the space station, a terrible accident happens?

Your tether rope to the ship gives way and you slowly drift away from the ship! First 50 feet away, then 100, then 100 yards and now a quarter mile. There are about 2 hours of oxygen in your tank and there is no hope of return. The communication system is out of range.

First, there is panic with wild attempts trying to swim back, yelling, and later crying for 20 minutes. Now exhausted and in silence you have only an hour left because you have used up so much oxygen.

Here is the plan that you determine to follow until death:
1. Give thanks to God for the life with which you've been blessed.
2. Go carefully over the plan of salvation which you have memorized in the past. Reconfirm Jesus is Lord of your life and ask for all sin to be forgiven.
3. Pray for all loved-ones with focused prayer for each.

4. Recite John 14 and put your name where appropriate.
5. Love God with all your heart, soul, mind, and strength until the oxygen runs out.
6. Enter eternity with Christ.

"Give thanks in all circumstances for this is God's will for you in Christ Jesus." 1 Thessalonians 5:17

There are four Spiritual laws for becoming saved:
1. Realize that God loves you. (John 3:16)
2. Realize that all have sinned and come short of the Glory of God. (Romans3:23).
3. Realize that Jesus died to remove our sins. (Romans 5:8)
4. Receive Jesus Christ as your Savior and Lord. (John 1:12) This 4th Law is crucial for becoming saved.

"That if you confess with your mouth, 'Jesus is Lord' and believe in your heart that God raised him from the dead, you will be saved...for everyone who calls on the name of the Lord will be saved." (Romans 10:9, 13)

"If we confess our sins, God is faithful and just and will forgive our sins and purify us from all unrighteousness." (1 John 1:9)

Receive Jesus as Savior and Lord. "Yet to all who received him, to those who believed in his name, he gave the right to become children of God. . ." (John 1:12)

"Do not be anxious about anything, but in everything, by prayer and petition, with thanksgiving, present your requests to God. And the peace of God, which transcends all understanding, will guard your hearts and your minds in Christ Jesus." (Philippians 4:6, 7)

"In my Father's house are many rooms; if it were not so, I would have told you. I am going there to prepare a place for you. And if I go and prepare a place for you, I will come back and take you to be with me that you also may be where I am." (John 14:2, 3)

"Jesus said, 'Love the Lord your God with all your heart and with all your soul and with all your mind.'" (Matthew 22:37)

"Precious in the sight of the Lord is the death of his saints." (Psalm 116:15)

What if, when we first enter Heaven, Jesus gives each of us an absolutely indescribable hug?

At the embrace we overflow with love and joy. There is peace and thrill beyond what we can imagine. We feel complete forgiveness. To feel our own personal relationship with Jesus finally culminated in a beautiful, wonderful, glorious, loving hug would be awesome!

First we hear; "Well done, good and faithful servant." Then we receive the HUG; wonderful beyond description! We feel our 'love tank" being filled to overflowing with gratitude and worship and so much more! The HUG instantly removes all pain, sorrow, greed, and pride! All selfishness, and martyr complexes wash away.

The "HUG" is just a vapor of time away for each one of us!

"He has taken me to the banquet hall, and his banner over me is love. Strengthen me with raisins, refresh me with apples, for I am faint with love. His left arm is under my head, and his right arm embraces me." (Song of Solomon 2:4-6)

"O Jerusalem, Jerusalem, you who kill the prophets and stone those sent to you, how often I have longed to gather your children together, as a hen gathers her chicks under her wings, but you were not willing." (Matthew 23:37)

"Whoever is wise, let him heed these things and consider the great love of the LORD." (Psalm 107:43)

"And the Lord has declared this day that you are his people, his treasured possession as he promised..." (Deuteronomy 26:18)

What if, in Heaven, there is a very special, beautiful experience for those who have had miscarried babies?

What if each of those miscarried embryos will have grown up in Heaven and are now patiently waiting for their parents to join them?

When their Christian parents arrive, they will see them fully mature in their spiritual bodies! Each parent will know and recognize their own miscarried children.

These miscarried throngs of adults are particularly pure and innocent and beautiful! They know God and His Grace more clearly than the rest of us who have been battle scarred during 'earth life.' These "miscarried adults" will have no loss from not having lived on earth. Instead they are perfect.

What if they are in Heaven now, waiting for their earthly parents to experience the most unusual surprise reunion beyond imagination? If you are one of those parents, anticipate the wondrous reunion with your miscarried sons and daughters allowed by God to enter Heaven very early in life through the shed blood of Jesus Christ!

"Before I formed you in the womb I knew you, before you were born I set you apart;" (Jeremiah 1:5)

"Jesus said, "Let the little children come to me, and do not hinder them, for the kingdom of heaven belongs to such as these."(Matthew 19:14)

"But now that he is dead, why should I fast? Can I bring him back again? I will go to him, but he will not return to me." (2 Samuel 12:23- King David's baby with Bathsheba)

"As soon as the sound of your greetings reached my ears, the baby in my womb(John the Baptist) leaped for joy. Blessed is she who has believed that what the Lord has said to her will be accomplished!" (Luke 1:44, 45) (Elizabeth speaking to Mary, Jesus' mother)

"Now to him who is able to do immeasurably more than all we ask or imagine, according to his power that is at work within us, to him be glory in the church and in Christ Jesus throughout all generations, for ever and ever! Amen." (Ephesians 3:20, 21)

"For nothing is impossible with God." (Luke 1:37)

"However, as it is written: 'No eye has seen, no ear has heard, no mind has conceived what God has prepared for those who love him." (1 Corinthians 2:9)

"Ask and it will be given to you; seek and you will find; knock and the door will be opened to you. For everyone who asks receives; he who seeks finds; and to him who knocks, the door will be opened." (Matthew 7:7, 8)

What if I died today?

The end would probably have been far more painless than I had imagined. Maybe just prior to death there would be a little panic and confusion. But this would flow into numbness, ejaculatory relaxation and peace followed quickly with exhilaration and that would be only the very beginning. The very best is yet to come! The following is a "possible agenda" for the first "day" in Heaven:

1. See God face to face.
2. Join the Saints and "bow the knee and confess Jesus is Lord."
3. Tour the Throne Room.
4. Thrill to experience a special get-together with loved ones.
5. Enjoy a spectacular revelation highlighting God's Glory and Magnificence.
6. See the incredible light show.
7. Partake of the hors de oeuvres before the Great Banquet Feast.
8. Return to the Throne Room—actually, we never really left it.
9. Attend the Book of Life Exhibit. All eyes are on the Father, Son, and Holy Spirit as they have an "Opening of the Book Ceremony." The Book opens by itself!

There is great joy as many are called to join the Lord. They leave with great honor and fanfare while being escorted into closeness to the Lord forevermore.

There is deep sorrow, however, among those whose names are missing from the Book of Life. All have experienced the Throne Room and the Lord face to face, confessed that Jesus is Lord and bowed their knee in worship. But it becomes painfully clear that it is too late for many. Those not listed in the book are grief struck and burdened beyond imagination. . .and transported away and down.

"Then I saw a great white throne and him who was seated on it. Earth and sky fled from his presence, and there was no place for them. And I saw the dead, great and small, standing before the throne, and books were opened. Another book was opened, which is the book of life. The dead were judged according to what they had done as recorded in the books. The sea gave up the dead that were in it, and death and Hades gave up the dead that were in them, and each person was judged according to what he had done. Then death and Hades were thrown into the lake of fire. The lake of fire is the second death. If anyone's name was not found written in the book of life, he was thrown into the lake of fire." (Revelation 20:11-15)

What if the nearer we get to God in Heaven, the greater our sheer joy and thrill?

When we enter Heaven, we will experience great joy. However, as we move closer and closer to God's throne, we will experience increasing levels of His awesome presence and glory. We will break out with spontaneous praise and worship! We move nearer for more!

Imagine combining every known pleasure available on planet earth into one full day of earth pleasure. Then compare "the earth-day pleasure" with one "Heaven-day pleasure." Without question, there would be no comparison. The "Heaven-day pleasure" would win hands down! In fact, the very best pleasures of earth spread over even a small portion of eternity would become quite boring. On the other hand, Heaven will never become boring in any way.

Why doesn't everybody on earth seek God with every fiber of their being? Heaven is awesome beyond our comprehension! Why are humans so distracted from the supremely important quest to enter into the Kingdom of Heaven for such poor pleasures that we seek so hard for on earth?

"You have made known to me the path of life; you will fill me with joy in your presence, with eternal pleasures at your right hand." (Psalm 16:11)

"Though you have not seen him, you love him; and even though you do not see him now, you believe in him and are filled with an inexpressible and glorious joy, for you are receiving the goal of your faith, the salvation of your souls." (1 Peter 1:8)

"Come near to God and he will come near to you." (James 4:8)

"Father, I want those you have given me to be with me where I am, and to see my glory, the glory you have given me because you loved me before the creation of the world." (John 17:24)

"At once I was in the Spirit, and there before me was a throne in heaven with someone sitting on it. And the one who sat there had the appearance of jasper and carnelian. A rainbow, resembling an emerald, encircled the throne. Surrounding the throne were twenty-four other thrones, and seated on them were twenty-four elders. They were dressed in white and had crowns of gold on their heads. From the throne came flashes of lightning, rumblings and peals of thunder." (Revelation 4:2-5)

"Then I looked and heard the voice of many angels, numbering thousands upon thousands, and ten thousand times ten thousand. They encircled the throne and the living creatures and the elders. In a loud voice they sang: "Worthy is the Lamb, who was slain, to receive power and wealth and wisdom and strength and honor and glory and praise!"

Then I heard every creature in heaven and on earth and under the earth and on the sea, and all that is in them, singing: "To him who sits on the throne and to the Lamb be praise and honor and glory and power, for ever and ever!" (Revelation 5:11-13)

"However, as it is written: 'No eye has seen, no ear has heard, no mind has conceived what God has prepared for those who love him.'" (1 Corinthians 2:9)

What if life is really very, very simple?

We humans frequently make life seem very complex and confusing. We confuse the simplicity of life with many distractions that really end up having nothing to do with our eternal destiny.

Here is life's simple recipe:
> Love God to the maximum.
> Love your "neighbor" to the maximum.

The simplicity of life is confused with the 7 deadly distractions which are: Pride, Lust, Gluttony, Envy, Laziness, Wrath, and Greed. These habits will deliver personal death easily in multiple ways over a lifetime.

Loving God and loving your neighbor will give you a wonderful life in this world and a spectacular life afterwards which is out of this world. Life is really so simple!

"Jesus replied: 'Love the Lord your God with all your heart and with all your soul and with all your mind. This is the first and greatest commandment. And the second is like it: 'Love your neighbor as yourself. All the Law and the Prophets hang on these two commandments.'" (Matthew 22:37-40)

"The acts of the sinful nature are obvious: sexual immorality, impurity and debauchery; idolatry and witchcraft; hatred, discord, jealousy, fits of rage, selfish ambition, dissensions, factions and envy; drunkenness, orgies, and the like. I warn you, as I did before, that those who live like this will not inherit the kingdom of God." (Galatians 5:19-21)

What if the admission price to get into Heaven is $1,000,000 (one million dollars)?

During a lifetime of 40 years of work, the average school teacher grosses around 3 million dollars. The above proposed price for admission into Heaven is far more expensive than most people could possibly accumulate during a lifetime.

The Bible states that the cost to gain admission into Heaven is a "commitment." A commitment to "Confess with your mouth that Jesus is Lord, and believe in your heart that God has raised Him from the dead. Then you will be saved." (Romans 10:9/10) This committant to gain entrance into Heaven costs nothing!

Why do so many people make such a poor financial decision regarding eternal life? It doesn't take an MBA to see a great value when it's offered!

"They replied, 'Believe in the Lord Jesus, and you will be saved—you and your household.'" (Acts 16:31)

"For whoever wants to save his life will lose it, but whoever loses his life for me will save it. What good is it for a man to gain the whole world, and yet lose or forfeit his very self?" (Luke 9:24, 25)

"I tell you, now is the time of God's favor, now is the day of salvation." (2 Corinthians 6:2)

"Though you have not seen him, you love him; and even though you do not see him now, you believe in him and are filled with an inexpressible and glorious joy, for you are receiving the goal of your faith, the salvation of your souls." (1 Peter 1:8, 9)

What if we could be 1/7th Christian and 6/7th non-Christian?

Is it possible to go through life being a partial Christian?

Being a "partial Christian" is quite popular these days it seems. Many "partial Christians" choose Sunday to act "Christianly", and the rest of the week to behave as non-Christians. Is it really possible to be a partial Christian?

Is being a Christian like being pregnant? We all understand that a woman is either completely pregnant or not pregnant at all. The size of the fetus doesn't really matter so much. There is no such thing as being partially pregnant, or being pregnant on Sundays and not pregnant the rest of the week. Just as pregnancy is all or none, so is it with Christianity. A person is either a Christian or a non-Christian.

Nevertheless, many Christians and non-Christians act like "partial Christians." Some people believe that if the Christian part of them is 51 percent or more, they will be judged as being fully Christian on Judgment Day. Just as it is uncomfortable to be half in the boat and half on the dock, so is the tension lived by "partial" Christians.

In God's eyes, we are either 100 percent Christian or not Christian at all. For Heaven's sake become a Christian and then live 100 percent like one. Partial Christianity just doesn't work and will eventually rob its victim of much joy and blessing. Almost being a Christian, like a near miss, doesn't get one into Heaven. It is impossible to have one foot in Heaven and one foot in Hell for eternity.

"No one can serve two masters. Either he will hate the one and love the other, or he will be devoted to the one and despise the other. You cannot serve both God and money. (Matthew 6:24)

"Therefore, I urge you, brothers, in view of God's mercy, to offer your bodies as living sacrifices, holy and pleasing to God—this is your spiritual act of worship. Do not conform any longer to the pattern of this world, but be transformed by the renewing of your mind. Then you will be able to test and approve what God's will is—his good, pleasing and perfect will." (Romans 12:1,2)

"We proclaim him, admonishing and teaching everyone with all wisdom, so that we may present everyone perfect in Christ." (Colossians 1:28)

"Be perfect, therefore, as your heavenly Father is perfect." (Matthew 5:48)

What if I am God's "Pleasure Unit Number - #12,000,000,001" (12 billion one), and I have been created specifically to give God great pleasure?

At my conversion, the Father sent His Holy Spirit to live inside of me. I am the temple that He lives in and, as such, the Holy Spirit experiences all that I experience. When I experience joy, the Holy Spirit inside of me, experiences that joy. A beautiful sunset or a wonderful meal gives me, and also the Holy Spirit living in me, pleasure. Because of the mystery of the Trinity, the Father and Jesus also experience what the Holy Spirit experiences in me!

Perhaps God has made each one of us to be vessels that He somehow lives in so that He can experience pleasure through us. What a privilege to be able to give God joy through our experience of good things! Our joy, laughter, and thrills all give God great joy. Of course, the opposite is also true. Our failures and sin grieve Him terribly.

Give the Lord a wonderful ride in your life. Fill your life with love, joy, and laughter. Flee from sin. God experiences what you experience!

"Do you not know that your body is a temple of the Holy Spirit who is in you, whom you have received from God? You are not your own; you were bought at a price. Therefore honor God with your body." (1 Corinthians 6:19, 20)

"... Christ in you, the hope of glory." (Colossians 1:27)

"But you know Him (The Spirit of Truth) for He lives with you and will be in you." (John 14:17) On that day you will realize that I am in my Father, and you are in me, and I am in you. (John 14:20)

"... Live as children of light (for the fruit of the light consists in all goodness, righteousness and truth) and find out what pleases the Lord." (Ephesians 5:9, 10).

(Authors note: There are approximately 7 billion people alive on earth now and it is estimated that one half of the people that have ever lived are alive at present.)

What if God decided that from now on He would "ZING" anyone immediately when that person sinned?

Perhaps the little "ZING" would be like a small lightning bolt focused on the offender precisely on the very part that was doing the sinning. The "ZING" would last one full second in an appropriate voltage from God and would probably be more intense than anyone would like. Most people experiencing the "ZING" would be knocked off their feet and dropped grimacing to the floor. After 1 second of "ZING," the person would completely recover without any bruises from the fall or residual damage from the "ZING." They would, however, have to get up from the floor.

Imagine a hand about to steal something or a tongue about to curse using God's Name receiving a one second lightning bolt to the offending fingers or tongue. Imagine one night-stands stopped at an embarrassing moment by a well-directed bolt. And, if an inappropriate attempt is tried a second time, the voltage is doubled!

There would be one thing for sure. Everyone would behave much better and there wouldn't be so many problems on planet earth!

At the present time, God's great mercy prevents the "ZING" from coming immediately at the time of the incident. In fact, it may be delayed until after judgment day.

"My son, do not make light of the Lord's discipline, and do not lose heart when he rebukes you, because the Lord disciplines those he loves, and he punishes everyone he accepts as a son." (Hebrews12:5, 6)

"I will punish the world for its evil, the wicked for their sins." (Isaiah 13:11)

"He will punish those who do not know God and do not obey the gospel of our Lord Jesus. They will be punished with everlasting destruction and shut out from the presence of the Lord and from the majesty of his power. . ." (2 Thessalonians 1:8, 9)

"I will punish you as your deeds deserve, declares the LORD. I will kindle a fire in your forests that will consume everything around you.'" (Jeremiah 21:14)

"Is it not from the mouth of the Most High that both calamities and good things come? Why should any living man complain when punished for his sins? Let us examine our ways and test them, and let us return to the LORD. (Lamentations 3:38-40)

What if we actually can enter into the hollow of God's hand?

It may be the perfect-sized place which is dome shaped with a finger roof and an entrance which opens and closes above God's mid-thumbs crossed over. Inside the hollow of God's hand, there is virtually no chance for enemies to come and harass us. Evil cannot penetrate or enter the hollow of God's hand. There is perfect warmth and protection. His hand provides a wonderful soft spot to curl up over the fourth finger leaning up against the fifth finger.

Climb into the hollow of God's hand whenever you want to! Just mellow out there a bit. It is always available. It's soft and comfy. There is no charge. There is free spiritual food to be enjoyed there which is out of this world. If you want silence, it's there. If you are lonely, there is someone very loving to talk to. It is a great place to make important decisions or just to fall off to sleep.

Go into the hollow of God's hand often in your prayer time!

"My sheep listen to my voice; I know them, and they follow me. I give them eternal life, and they shall never perish; no one can snatch them out of my hand. My Father, who has given them to me, is greater than all; no one can snatch them out of my Father's hand. I and the Father are one." (John 10:27-29)

"If the LORD delights in a man's way, he makes his steps firm; though he stumble, he will not fall, for the LORD upholds him with his hand. (Psalm 37:23, 24)

"Because you are my help, I sing in the shadow of your wings. My soul clings to you; your right hand upholds me." (Psalm 63:7, 8

"Yet, O LORD, you are our Father. We are the clay, you are the potter; we are all the work of your hand." (Isaiah 64:8)

"The LORD upholds all those who fall and lifts up all who are bowed down. The eyes of all look to you, and you give them their food at the proper time. You open your hand and satisfy the desires of every living thing." (Psalm 145:14-16)

"My times are in your hands; deliver me from my enemies and from those who pursue me." (Psalm 31:15)

What if there are two chapters before Genesis 1 in the Bible that at present are unknown to us?

These 2 chapters would explain and answer the "WHY" question that we humans wonder so much about. Why is there so much pain and suffering if God loves us so much and is all-powerful?

Job, in the book titled Job, didn't have access to the first two chapters in the book about him. If he could have read those chapters, he would have understood what God was doing with his life and why God was allowing all those troubles into his life.

Perhaps the two chapters before Genesis 1 that we don't have access to would explain topics such as why God created Satan to tempt us and how Satan became the "prince of this world." These chapters would clarify how God is using Satan to accomplish His perfect goals for each one of us. They would explain why Satan's job description is to "sift" humans and why bad things happen to good people.

The answer might be as simple for us as it was for Job. Perhaps Satan has told God that Christians want to be Christians because of all the benefits Christians get and not because they love God. Perhaps God is proving to Satan that Christians are willing to give up everything, even life itself, in order to love God with all their heart, soul, mind, and strength!

"On another day the angels came to present themselves before the LORD, and Satan also came with them to present himself before him. And the LORD said to Satan, "Where have you come from?"

Satan answered the LORD, "From roaming through the earth and going back and forth in it." Then the LORD said to Satan, "Have you considered my servant Job? There is no one on earth like him; he is blameless and upright, a man who fears God and shuns evil. And he still maintains his integrity, though you incited me against him to ruin him without any reason." "Skin for skin!" Satan replied. "A man will give all he has for his own life. But stretch out your hand and strike his flesh and bones, and he will surely curse you to your face." The LORD said to Satan, "Very well, then, he is in your hands; but you must spare his life."

So Satan went out from the presence of the LORD and afflicted Job with painful sores from the soles of his feet to the top of his head." (Job 2:1-7)

"Simon, Simon, Satan has asked to sift you as wheat. But I have prayed for you, Simon, that your faith may not fail. And when you have turned back, strengthen your brothers." But he replied, "Lord, I am ready to go with you to prison and to death." Jesus answered, "I tell you, Peter, before the rooster crows today, you will deny three times that you know me." (Luke 22:31-34)

"The LORD your God is testing you to find out whether you love him with all your heart and with all your soul. It is the LORD your God you must follow, and him you must revere. Keep his commands and obey him; serve him and hold fast to him." (Deuteronomy 13:3, 4)

What if God is using planet earth as a "boot camp" to select out a strong group of humans that will be adopted into His family and live with Him forever?

Each individual in this select group would need to make a personal choice asking Christ to be 'Lord of their life' and to follow Jesus no matter what the cost, even to death. Entrance into the select group is free and not related to wisdom, wealth, or strength. At the end of time this huge, select group will be ushered into the Kingdom of God with glorious joy to love and enjoy God forever.

At present, however, God has allowed Satan, in the role of a very mean military sergeant, to tempt and discourage as many of the participants as possible. Satan has been given authority to use wealth, pride, anger, power, disease, along with many other temptations, to deceive prospective applicants away from trying to get into God's intimate family.

All participants have access to God's free power to resist Satan causing him to flee. They, furthermore, are given the ability to bind any strongman that Satan has in his kingdom in order to release Satan's captives. Each candidate faces one lifetime of spiritual battles tailor made by Satan to keep him or her away from God.

Take up the armor of God as mentioned in Ephesians 6 and fight for all you are worth. The Lord has already won the battle!

"The LORD your God is testing you to find out whether you love him with all your heart and with all your soul. It is the Lord your God you must follow, and him you must revere. Keep his commands and obey him; serve him and hold fast to him." (Deuteronomy 13:3, 4)

"You, dear children, are from God and have overcome them, because the one who is in you is greater than the one who is in the world." (1 John 4:4)

"Be bold, be courageous, do not be discouraged, do not be disappointed, for I the Lord your God am with you wherever you go." (Joshua 1:9)

"The thief comes only to steal and kill and destroy; I have come that they may have life, and have it to the full." (John 10:10)

"The reason the Son of God appeared was to destroy the devil's work." (1 John 3:8)

"Therefore, since we are surrounded by such a great cloud of witnesses, let us throw off everything that hinders and the sin that so easily entangles, and let us run with perseverance the race marked out for us. Let us fix our eyes on Jesus, the author and perfecter of our faith, who for the joy set before him endured the cross, scorning its shame, and sat down at the right hand of the throne of God. Consider him who endured such opposition from sinful men, so that you will not grow weary and lose heart. In your struggle against sin, you have not yet resisted to the point of shedding your blood." (Hebrews 12:1-4)

What if there are no job openings in Heaven available for mechanics, plumbers, cooks, or house help?

No janitor, truck driver, waitress or similar jobs are available. There are no openings for garbage haulers, attorneys or doctors.

BUT

There is a severe shortage of people to occupy the roles of princesses and princes. There are an abundance of openings for Kings, Queens, Premiers, rulers, overseers, orchestra conductors, special food tasters, and the like beyond our imaginative thrill. Furthermore, no experience is necessary and once the job is applied for, the acceptance is guaranteed without even having an interview.

Heaven is a wonderful place to go and work! Apply now for entrance!

"Peter answered him, "We have left everything to follow you! What then will there be for us?" Jesus said to them, "I tell you the truth, at the renewal of all things, when the Son of Man sits on his glorious throne, you who have followed me will also sit on twelve thrones, judging the twelve tribes of Israel. And everyone who has left houses or brothers or sisters or father or mother or children or fields for my sake will receive a hundred times as much and will inherit eternal life." (Matthew 19:27-29)

"You are those who have stood by me in my trials. And I confer on you a kingdom, just as my Father conferred one on me, so that you may eat and drink at my table in my kingdom and sit on thrones, judging the twelve tribes of Israel." (Luke 22:28-30)

"However, as it is written: 'No eye has seen, no ear has heard, no mind has conceived what God has prepared for those who love him. . .' " (1 Corinthians 2:9)

What if there were a price that, if paid, you would do something very, very wrong?

What is your price? Would it be $1,000 or $1 million dollars? Would it be $1 billion to cause you to give in, do the deed, and accept the "free" money? Achan's price was a purple robe, 200 pieces of silver, and a gold bar. (Joshua 7:20-22) King David's price was a pretty lady. Pilate's price was popularity. Judas' price was only 30 pieces of silver!

Every person may have a certain price above which the person can no longer resist the temptation. Always be aware of 'your price' and if the temptation gets close to it, flee before your price is met and you fall for the temptation.

"Be self-controlled and alert. Your enemy the devil prowls around like a roaring lion looking for someone to devour. Resist him, standing firm in the faith, because you know that your brothers throughout the world are undergoing the same kind of sufferings." (1 Peter 5:8, 9)

"And lead us not into temptation, but deliver us from the evil one." (Matthew 6:13)

"...choose for yourselves this day whom you will serve...but as for me and my household, we will serve the Lord." (Joshua 24:15)

"Watch and pray so that you will not fall into temptation. The spirit is willing, but the body is weak." (Matthew 26:41)

"No temptation has seized you except what is common to man. And God is faithful; he will not let you be tempted beyond what you can bear. But when you are tempted, he will also provide a way out so that you can stand up under it." (1 Corinthians 10:13)

What if Heaven is actually not a big long boring church service that drones on forever?

What if Heaven, instead, is thrill and adventure! What if every day in heaven gets better and better the longer you are there? There is overflowing love and joy and excitement. There is rest and exhilaration. There is great anticipation with overwhelming satisfaction. God's glory and majesty will thrill us in ever increasing amounts, more than any earthly pleasure could ever do. And all that is just in the first bit of Heaven with much more to come. There is so, so much more!

In Heaven, we will realize that God is the Creator of everything that we have ever desired. He is the provider of all we could possibly want. The closer we get to our Creator, the greater we will experience "all we have ever desired" and that is just the very beginning!

SEEK GOD HARD! You will not believe what He is planning for you!

"However, as it is written: 'No eye has seen, no ear has heard, no mind has conceived what God has prepared for those who love him' "...(1 Corinthians 2:9)

"Praise be to the God and Father of our Lord Jesus Christ, who has blessed us in the heavenly realms with every spiritual blessing in Christ." (Ephesians 1:3)
"You have made known to me the path of life; you will fill me with joy in your presence with eternal pleasures at your right hand." (Psalm 16:11),

"Praise be to the God and Father of our Lord Jesus Christ! In his great mercy he has given us new birth into a living hope through the resurrection of Jesus Christ from the dead, and into an inheritance that can never perish, spoil or fade—kept in heaven for you,. . ."(1 Peter:3,4)

"Blessed are those who are persecuted because of righteousness, for theirs is the kingdom of heaven. Blessed are you when people insult you, persecute you and falsely say all kinds of evil against you because of me. Rejoice and be glad, because great is your reward in heaven," (Matthew 5:11, 12)

What if, during this short life on earth, we each determine our fate for eternity?

Choosing between Heaven or Hell is the biggest decision of our earthly life!

Many people choose Heaven during the first 12 years of life when they are mere youth. That simple decision determines unfathomable riches and blessings for them forever. Many others choose Heaven because of difficult circumstances that prompt them to seek God for help. When they look back from Heaven they will be so thankful for the disaster in their life which caused such a wonderful result.

It is sad that because of procrastination many people just don't get around to choosing Heaven. Some die unexpectedly and are surprised to enter eternity so quickly before making "the decision". Others wait too long and become too senile to make a decision. Some have misleading information and opt to "go with the flow" when the flow was going the wrong direction away from Heaven. Make sure that you don't miss heaven for the world. Choose Heaven today.

"I tell you, now is the time of God's favor, now is the day of salvation." (2 Corinthians 6:2)

"But if serving the Lord seems undesirable to you, then choose for yourselves this day whom you will serve, whether the gods your forefathers served beyond the River, or the gods of the Amorites, in whose land you are living. But as for me and my household, we will serve the Lord." (Joshua 14:15)

"These have come so that your faith—of greater worth than gold, which perishes even though refined by fire—may be proved genuine and may result in praise, glory and honor when Jesus Christ is revealed. Though you have not seen him, you love him; and even though you do not see him now, you believe in him and are filled with an inexpressible and glorious joy, for you are receiving the goal of your faith, the salvation of your souls." (1 Peter 1:7-9)

Only one life will soon be past.
Only what's done for Christ will last.

What if, for each day we are alive on planet earth, we live a corresponding one million years in heaven?

Then we return to live our next day on earth, followed by returning to glorious Heaven for another million years. On and on the cycle goes until we eventually grow old on earth, die and then go to Heaven forever. Compared to eternity, life on earth is so short!

From Heaven's eternal perspective, life on earth is a rare and precious experience and would seem to be a mere vapor of mist that is quickly over. After one million years in Heaven, how would you spend the next 24 hours on earth after which you would return to Heaven for another million Heaven years?

I would suggest spending it this way--

Get up early and spend time with the Lord committing the day to Him. (You will be returning to Him soon.)

Reach out to those you love the most and love them toward God as much as possible.

Maximize "good works" with whatever abilities you might have.

Other very popular choices are: sleep late, have a lazy breakfast, read the paper, lunch, nap, TV, and computer time followed by bed.

Our earthly lives are a short vapor! Make a big puff for Jesus every day and don't waste the earthly possibilities when you can lay up treasure instead!

"Why, you do not even know what will happen tomorrow. What is your life? You are a mist that appears for a little while and then vanishes." (James 4:14)

"By faith Moses, when he had grown up, refused to be known as the son of Pharaoh's daughter. He chose to be mistreated along with the people of God rather than to enjoy the pleasures of sin for a short time. He regarded disgrace for the sake of Christ as of greater value than the treasures of Egypt, because he was looking ahead to his reward." (Hebrews 11:24-26)

"Do not store up for yourselves treasures on earth, where moth and rust destroy, and where thieves break in and steal. But store up for yourselves treasures in heaven, where moth and rust do not destroy, and where thieves do not break in and steal. For where your treasure is, there your heart will be also." (Matthew 6:19-21)

"How long will you lie there, you sluggard? When will you get up from your sleep? A little sleep, a little slumber, a little folding of the hands to rest and poverty will come on you like a bandit and scarcity like an armed man." (Proverbs 6:9-11)

What if our life on earth is just a quick quiz or test that we take from our loving God?

To us, the test might seem a long 80 years, more or less, but to the Lord, it is just a quick test that He administers.

The terms of the quiz are Pass/Fail. Those who pass, go into eternal life with God in Heaven. Those who fail go into eternal life without God in Hell.

All participants in the testing program begin as sinners and continue to sin to various degrees; some tally minimal sins of minor degree and others log huge amounts of sin during their lifetimes. The crucial point of the test is to become totally sinless. That is, any sin, even a small one, results in a "fail". To pass God's test, participants are required to be completely sinless!

To become sinless is totally free and all test participants have this option to choose to have their sins completely removed. Sin removal is easy and involves asking Jesus Christ to forgive one's sin prior to death and to trust in Jesus Christ's grace to give them a passing score. To become sinless is not dependent on the test participant's wealth, power, fame, or intelligence.

Furthermore, to pass is not related to a participant's goodness or sinfulness. To pass is only dependent on each participant's faith in Jesus Christ to forgive their sins and be Lord in his or her life.

Life is a little test!

"If we confess our sins, he is faithful and just and will forgive us our sins and purify us from all unrighteousness." (1 John 1:9)

"For it is by grace you have been saved, through faith—and this not from yourselves, it is the gift of God—not by works, so that no one can boast." (Ephesians 2:8, 9)

"That if you confess with your mouth, 'Jesus is Lord,' and believe in your heart that God raised him from the dead, you will be saved." (Romans 10:9)

"They replied, "Believe in the Lord Jesus, and you will be saved—you and your household." (Acts 16:31)

"Why, you do not even know what will happen tomorrow. What is your life? You are a mist that appears for a little while and then vanishes." (James 4:14)

What if you gained the whole world, but lost your soul?

The wealth of the world is probably trillions of trillions of dollars. Imagine that you own all the diamonds, gold, property, oil; everything is yours! You owned the whole world for one lifetime of 80 or 90 years, but afterwards you forfeited your soul!

80 years of pure luxury on earth has been traded for an eternity of hell. You missed the wonderful future life in heaven with God. All hope is gone forever.

To gain the whole world but eventually lose one's soul is a disaster. Don't make such a foolish choice and for sure, DON'T MISS HEAVEN FOR THE WORLD!

"What good will it be for a man if he gains the whole world, yet forfeits his soul? Or what can a man give in exchange for his soul? For the Son of Man is going to come in his Father's glory with his angels, and then he will reward each person according to what he has done." (Matthew 16:26, 27)

"There was a rich man who was dressed in purple and fine linen and lived in luxury every day. At his gate was laid a beggar named Lazarus, covered with sores and longing to eat what fell from the rich man's table. Even the dogs came and licked his sores. The time came when the beggar died and the angels carried him to Abraham's side. The rich man also died and was buried. In hell, where he was in torment, he looked up and saw Abraham far away, with Lazarus by his side. So he called to him, 'Father Abraham, have pity on me and send Lazarus to dip the tip of his finger in water and cool my tongue, because I am in agony in this fire.'

But Abraham replied, 'Son, remember that in your lifetime you received your good things, while Lazarus received bad things, but now he is comforted here and you are in agony. And besides all this, between us and you a great chasm has been fixed, so that those who want to go from here to you cannot, nor can anyone cross over from there to us." (Luke 16:19-26)

What if Jesus came to us wearing modern clothing and no robes at all?

Blue jeans — probably not designer — a nice manly shirt, leather brown belt, nice sneakers (I'll not tell you which brand He prefers). He has a wallet with 1 credit card and some cash; there are keys in His right pocket. He wears his hair slightly long almost to His shoulders.

Would you recognize Him as Jesus? Or would you be like Cleopas and the other disciple on the Emmaus road that walked and talked together with Jesus without knowing that it was actually Him? They knew that Jesus had just died and obviously wouldn't be walking with them. For Cleopas, Jesus needed to "break bread" with him before he knew it was Jesus. Then he knew it was Jesus without any doubt.

If Jesus were walking alongside you and me one day, we also would assume that it couldn't be the real Jesus. Only when Jesus revealed Himself to us would we realize that this was Jesus! Then our hearts would be strangely warmed with the thrill of the moment.

Keep alert. It is possible that Jesus might join you on your next walk. No matter how Jesus dresses, He casually might come alongside you and speak to you. Don't miss Him because of your unbelief. You will recognize Him sooner or later because you know Him.

"Now that same day two of them were going to a village called Emmaus, about seven miles from Jerusalem. They were talking with each other about everything that had happened. As they talked and discussed these things with each other, Jesus himself came up and walked along with them; but they were kept from recognizing him." Luke 24:13-15)

"When he was at the table with them, he took bread, gave thanks, broke it and began to give it to them. Then their eyes were opened and they recognized him, and he disappeared from their sight. They asked each other, "Were not our hearts burning within us while he talked with us on the road and opened the Scriptures to us?" (Luke 24:30-32)

"My sheep listen to my voice; I know them, and they follow me." (John 10:27)

"Then the righteous will answer him, Lord, when did we see you hungry and feed you, or thirsty and give you something to drink? When did we see you a stranger and invite you in, or needing clothes and clothe you? When did we see you sick or in prison and go to visit you?" "The King will reply, "I tell you the truth, whatever you did for one of the least of these brothers of mine, you did for me." (Matthew 25:37-40)

What if Jesus, instead of dying on the cross, died of old age?

Imagine that He had a successful full life of ministry speaking, teaching, and modeling the Christian life. Eventually, He died a natural death at a very old age. Imagine there were no beatings by Pilate and no crucifixion. Imagine that He died of old age instead of dying on the cross!

Unfortunately for us, we would have no way to permanently get rid of our sins! Without Christ's death on the cross, we would still need to sacrifice sheep, goats, and pigeons regularly to temporarily cleanse ourselves from sin. We are so fortunate that Christ died on the cross to save us from our sins once and for all!

Praise God that for the joy set before Him, Jesus endured the cross. God's way is always best!

"Let us fix our eyes on Jesus, the author and perfecter of our faith, who for the joy set before him endured the cross, scorning its shame, and sat down at the right hand of the throne of God." (Hebrews 12:2)

"For Christ died for sins once for all, the righteous for the unrighteous, to bring you to God." (1 Peter 3:18)

"And if Christ has not been raised, your faith is futile; you are still in your sins. Then those also who have fallen asleep in Christ are lost. If only for this life we have hope in Christ, we are to be pitied more than all men. But Christ has indeed been raised from the dead, the first fruits of those who have fallen asleep. For since death came through a man, the resurrection of the dead comes also through a man. For as in Adam all die, so in Christ all will be made alive." (1 Corinthians 15:17-22)

What if at birth each human is freely given the following "package"?

A billion-dollar brain.
A billion-dollar heart.
A billion-dollar nerve system.
A billion-dollar muscular body equipped with skeleton of varying sizes especially created for each individual.
A billion-dollar digestive system.
A billion-dollar skin system which self renews itself every 7 years?
A billion-dollar "beautification process" with unique hair, dimples, freckles, and special features of varying sizes and colors?

There you have it! At birth, the final cost analysis for your body is approximately $7 billion dollars and your body is programmed to run efficiently for 70 or 80 years of active, fun-filled life.

Why would anyone feed this miraculous $7 billion body toxic doses of beer and whiskey that gums up the finely tuned liver and brain? Why would anyone smoke cigarettes that will shorten the body's life span by 10 years on an average? Why would anyone in their right mind drive drunk and risk smashing a $7 billion body in one drunken fling?

Some people are either really foolish or very stupid!

"So God created man in his own image, in the image of God he created him; male and female he created them." (Genesis 1:27)

"For you created my inmost being; you knit me together in my mother's womb. I praise you because I am fearfully and wonderfully made." (Psalm 139:13,14)

"Do you not know that your body is a temple of the Holy Spirit, who is in you, whom you have received from God? You are not your own; you were bought at a price. Therefore honor God with your body." (1 Corinthians 6:19, 20)

"For we are God's workmanship, created in Christ Jesus to do good works, which God prepared in advance for us to do." (Ephesians 2:10)

What if salvation is much easier than we can imagine?

Many people have a hard time believing that salvation is so simple! We analyze "salvation" and break it down into multiple complexities.. We struggle and speculate and work different angles. Perhaps salvation is far simpler than we think.

Salvation requires a very small amount of faith! Doubts may be huge in the midst of "a small amount of faith." Fortunately it is not the amount of doubt that matters. Only a small amount of faith is required.

 The faith needed may be as little as a person whispering, "Help me, Jesus. I need you. Please save me." It is so simple!

At the point of salvation, the Holy Spirit miraculously enters the seeker. The person then experiences the Lord and this relationship deepens as time progresses. Eventually the person apologizes for past deeds and gives thanks to God for giving salvation to him or her. Over a lifetime, the new Christian grows the "small amount of faith" into a "mountain-moving faith."

All it took initially was "a small amount of faith" even though it was positioned in a large bed of doubt. With that simple little step of faith, huge miraculous things happened. "Therefore you become a new creature, the old things are gone; all things are made new." (2 Corinthians 5:17)

Salvation is not meant to be difficult or strenuous. Salvation is not like climbing an impossible mountain. It is meant to be easy and the Lord offers it freely. Salvation is amazing. It is quick and free to all who desire it and it lasts forever!

"Believe on the Lord Jesus Christ and you will be saved and your house." Acts 16:31

"That if you confess with your mouth, 'Jesus is Lord,' and believe in your heart that God raised him from the dead, you will be saved." Romans 10:9

"Therefore if anyone is in Christ, he is a new creature. The old has gone; the new has come." (2 Corinthians 5:17)

"Yet to all who received Him, to those who believed in His name, He gave the right to become children of God. . ." (John 1:12)

What if all of Satan's temptations were very ugly and stupid and yucky and boring and hard work and smelly at the outset and unpleasant to the eyes?

What if the temptations hurt and stung and cost a lot of money? What if it was obvious that the temptations were clearly sent directly from an awful, angry, deceiver who never, ever would give a good deal?

If that were the case, life would be so much better! We wouldn't get into so much trouble, that's for sure. Life probably would be altogether thrilling, peaceful, and absolutely wonderful!

Unfortunately for us, Satan wraps his temptations with eye-appealing packages. Some of them walk and smile. Some feel good. Others taste good. All of them result in disaster and eventually hurt us terribly.

Pray to God for serious discernment and power to avoid Satan's pretty little packages.

"Then the LORD God said to the woman, 'What is this you have done?' The woman said, 'The serpent deceived me, and I ate.'" Genesis 3:13

"Be self-controlled and alert. Your enemy the devil prowls around like a roaring lion looking for someone to devour." (1 Peter 5:8)

"At one time we too were foolish, disobedient, deceived, and enslaved by all kinds of passions and pleasures. We lived in malice and envy, being hated and hating one another." (Titus 3:3)

"Lead us not into temptation and deliver us from evil." (Matt. 6:13)

"I will direct you always." (Isaiah 58:11)

What if "God hurts those deeply whom He loves dearly?"

Pain and suffering are very effective tools that God uses carefully to give us great blessings. God is very loving and would not want to cause us any pain needlessly. But pain may be the best tool that God can use to draw us closer to Himself. Precisely directed pain or suffering from God's loving hand may be the perfect stimulus to propel us toward God as quickly as we can go.

Pain often is the best method to help a rich person kneel before God in humility. Pain or suffering may be the least painful treatment available to soften the "Scrooge" in each one of us.

At times, pain and suffering are in the physical or emotional realm. Other times the pain may be in the spiritual realm. No matter in which realm we experience pain or suffering, it may be the sharpest, most accurate method that God carefully uses to draw us closer to the Himself!

Pain and suffering are wonderful tools in God's loving hands. No other gift will work as quickly and as well.

"For our light and momentary troubles are achieving for us an eternal glory that far outweighs them all." (2 Corinthians 4:17)

"Consider it pure joy, my brothers, whenever you face trials of many kinds, because you know that the testing of your faith develops perseverance. Perseverance must finish its work so that you may be mature and complete, not lacking anything." (James 1:2-4)

"When times are good, be happy; but when times are bad, consider; God has made the one as well as the other." (Ecclesiastes 7:14)

Dear friends, do not be surprised at the painful trial you are suffering, as though something strange were happening to you. But rejoice that you participate in the sufferings of Christ, so that you may be overjoyed when his glory is revealed. (1 Peter 4:12,13)

"Not only so, but we also rejoice in our sufferings, because we know that suffering produces perseverance; perseverance, character; and character, hope. And hope does not disappoint us, because God has poured out his love into our hearts by the Holy Spirit, whom he has given us." (Romans 5:2-5)

"I consider that our present sufferings are not worth comparing with the glory that will be revealed in us." (Romans 8:18)

What if your prayer time is the most important and significant part of your life?

We celebrate birthdays and graduations as very significant events; baby showers, wedding showers, and anniversaries rank high as well.

However, one's ordinary prayer time is probably the most significant activity in anyone's life. That is not to say that birthdays and anniversaries are not important in God's eyes. They are. It is just that prayer of any intensity is so much more significant and "earth shaking!"

A moment or two of prayer spent talking to the Creator of the Universe is huge in significant value. To communicate personally with God who easily made trillions of complex galaxies is an amazing opportunity and privilege. A moment with God in prayer is far more significant than any earthly celebration or activity accomplished without relating to God. Prayer unleashes God's power.

Why not do something really significant today!

"I tell you the truth, if you have faith as small as a mustard seed, you can say to this mountain, 'Move from here to there' and it will move. Nothing will be impossible for you." Matthew 17:20

"The Lord delights in the prayers of the upright." (Proverbs 15:8)

"If you remain in me and my words remain in you, ask whatever you wish and it will be given you." (John 15:7)

"The prayer of a righteous man is powerful and effective." (James 4:16)

"Pray continually." (1 Thessalonians 5:17)

"Then he returned to his disciples and found them sleeping. 'Couldn't you men keep watch with me for one hour?'" he asked Peter. [41] "Watch and pray so that you will not fall into temptation. The spirit is willing, but the flesh is weak." (Matthew 26:40,41)

"Devote yourselves to prayer with an alert mind and a thankful heart." (Colossians 4:2)

What if our total goal and purpose on planet earth is to "lay up treasure in Heaven"?

Many people feel that laying up treasure for ourselves in Heaven is too hedonistic. It's prideful and greedy. It might make others feel badly if we have a lot more treasure than others have. And besides, we will give our treasure to Jesus in the first five minutes in Heaven and then it's gone for eternity. Lastly, our treasure in Heaven would be distracting to the real purpose of Heaven which is loving the Lord and Him only.

This "low" impression of treasure in Heaven needs to revisited. What if the "treasure" that Christ talks about isn't pearls and gold and crowns as most people suppose the treasure to be? "Treasure in Heaven" may be the ability to know the Lord more clearly and love Him more dearly! Perhaps "treasure" really is "closeness to God" This treasure is not a distraction or a temporary pleasure gone quickly. The treasure is "more of Jesus."

The Lord commands us to lay up treasure in Heaven by doing two types of good works--
    1. Love God while we are down here on earth.
    2. Love others with the love the Lord gives us.

Christ commands us to lay up treasure in Heaven and the reward probably is more of Jesus Christ Himself! Don't be miserly in your desire to lay up treasure in Heaven. More of God is your reward!

"Store your treasures in heaven, where moths and rust cannot destroy, and thieves do not break in and steal. Wherever your treasure is, there the desires of your heart will also be. (Matthew 6:20, 21)

"Be happy about it! Be very glad! For a great reward awaits you in Heaven." (Matthew 5:12)

"But when you pray, go away by yourself, shut the door behind you, and pray to your Father in private. Then your Father, who sees everything, will reward you." (Matthew 6:6)

"Do not throw away this confident trust in the Lord. Remember the great reward it brings you! (Hebrews 10:35)

"Come near to God and he will come near to you. Wash your hands, you sinners, and purify your hearts." James 4:8

"Serve wholeheartedly, as if you were serving the Lord, not men, because you know that the Lord will reward everyone for whatever good he does, whether he is slave or free." (Ephesians 6:7, 8)

"Jesus replied: Love the Lord your God with all your heart and with all your soul and with all your mind." Matthew 22:37)

What if the four most powerful words that we humans can possibly say are "Lord, I Love You!"?

What happens if we do that? It takes only a second or two to accomplish this little task.

It is just possible that the angels in Heaven stop all that they are doing and agree in unison with your bold statement. Thousands of thousands of angels worship and love God along with you in total unison. The rocks cry out in agreement. The trees clap their hands and shake in agreement. Lightning and thunder smash, crack, and explode in joyous praise.

A huge treasure gets laid up in heaven in your account! All for just one simple heart felt "I Love You, Lord" here on earth during a busy day filled with mundane tasks that seem never to end.

Do something really significant and say--"Lord, I Love You!"

"Jesus replied, 'You must love the Lord your God with all your heart, all your soul, and all your mind. This is the first and greatest commandment.'" (Matthew 22:37) (Deuteronomy 6:4)

"And now these three remain: faith, hope and love. But the greatest of these is love." (1 Corinthians 13:13)

"Hatred stirs up dissension, but love covers over all wrongs." (Proverbs 10:12)

"Let the rivers clap their hands, Let the mountains sing together for joy; let them sing before the LORD, for he comes to judge the earth." (Psalm 98:8)

"You will go out in joy and be led forth in peace; the mountains and hills will burst into song before you, and all the trees of the field will clap their hands." (Isaiah 55:12)

What if Satan revealed himself clearly to you?

Would you be a better Christian in order to protect yourself from him? Many people fear Satan more than they believe in God, the Creator of Satan. Satan's existence is powerful evidence for the spiritual world and the troubles that we each face.

Satan's existence and plan of operation are clearly evident. Take heart that the battle with him "is won but not yet."

"Now the serpent was more crafty than any of the wild animals the Lord God had made. He said to the woman, 'Did God really say, 'You must not eat from any tree in the garden?'" (Genesis 3:1)

"The great dragon was hurled down—that ancient serpent called the devil, or Satan, who leads the whole world astray. He was hurled to the earth, and his angels with him." (Revelation 12:9)

"He replied, 'I saw Satan fall like lightning from heaven. I have given you authority to trample on snakes and scorpions and to overcome all the power of the enemy; nothing will harm you." (Luke 10:18,19)

"The reason the Son of God appeared was to destroy the devil's work" (1 John 3:8)

"Be self-controlled and alert. Your enemy the devil prowls around like a roaring lion looking for someone to devour. Resist him, standing firm in the faith because you know that your brothers throughout the world are undergoing the same kind of sufferings." (1 Peter 5:8, 9)

"Put on the full armor of God so that you can take your stand against the devil's schemes. For our struggle is not against flesh and blood, but against the rulers, against the authorities, against the powers of this dark world and against the spiritual forces of evil in the heavenly realms." (Ephesians 6:11, 12)

"And the devil, who deceived them, was thrown into the lake of burning sulfur, where the beast and the false prophet had been thrown. They will be tormented day and night for ever and ever." (Revelation 20:10)

What if God had placed the Tree of the Knowledge of Good and Evil in the furthest away spot in the Garden of Eden on top of a mountain where it is terribly difficult to get to?

It's a place surrounded by icy slippery glaciers and rocky crags. It is not a nice place and Adam and Eve would never want to venture there.

Then, what if God made the fruit on this tree prickly with a hard outer shell needing a big rock to crack it? The "fruit" smells putrid and looks even worse. What if, in addition, the evil contents inside were very small and hard to find?

If God would have hidden the Tree of Good and Evil in a terribly difficult spot to find instead of "the middle of the garden," perhaps the fall of mankind by Adam and Eve would not have happened so soon. If the fruit were not "pleasing to the eye" perhaps the fall might not have occurred even by now. Then, the love story between God and mankind living happily together without sin might still be continuing on.

But, God placed the tree in the center of the garden and He made the fruit pleasing to the eye!

God's ways are so far above our ways. His wisdom we cannot always understand. But we know we need to humbly bow very low before our Creator and worship Him. Our task is to love Him with all we can muster in the midst of temptation and difficulties. We are reassured that everything is proceeding exactly according to God's perfect plan.

"God saw all that he had made, and it was very good." (Genesis 1:31)

"In the middle of the garden were the tree of life and the tree of the knowledge of good and evil." (Genesis 2:9)

"And the LORD God commanded the man, 'You are free to eat from any tree in the garden; but you must not eat from the tree of the knowledge of good and evil, for when you eat of it you will surely die.'" (Genesis 2:16,17)

"When the woman saw that the fruit of the tree was good for food and pleasing to the eye, and also desirable for gaining wisdom, she took some and ate it. She also gave some to her husband, who was with her, and he ate it." (Genesis 3:6)

"When times are good, be happy; but when times are bad, consider: God has made the one as well as the other." (Ecclesiastes 7:4)

"Our God is in heaven; He does whatever pleases him." (Psalm 115:3)

"As the heavens are higher than the earth, so are my ways higher than your ways and my thoughts than your thoughts." (Isaiah 55:9)

"As for God, his way is perfect; the word of the LORD is flawless." (Psalm 18:30)

"Who has understood the mind of the Lord, or instructed Him as His counselor? (Isaiah 40:13)

What if each "minor" sin costs a sinner $25 to get forgiven?

A gossipy comment, a lusty look, a "lazy failure to help" costs somewhere between $75 and $100. What if every sin was ranked on a scale of 1-10 with 1 being "minor" and 10 being "treason."

If all of the sins which one person committed during a lifetime were plotted on a graph, they would probably form a bell-shaped curve shaped like a small hill. The majority of sins would hopefully be skewed into the "minor" to "moderate" severity sin groupings. The "average" sins would probably be in the $50 to $500 range per sin, but some cost $500,000.

A 70-year-old male living in America would probably be in the $100 million debt range! To get into Heaven, one must be completely sinless and totally debt free!

Get'm forgiven fast, NOW before inflation makes the sum even worse!

"Be perfect, therefore, as your heavenly Father is perfect." (Matthew 5:48)

"Because of the Lord's love for us we are not consumed, for his compassions never fail." (Lamentations 3:22)

"Forgive us our debts, as we also have forgiven our debtors. And lead us not into temptation, but deliver us from the evil one." (Matthew 6:12)

"If you confess your sin, God is just and will forgive the sin and cleanse you from all unrighteousness." (1 John 1:9)

"In Him, we have redemption through his blood, the forgiveness of sins, in accordance with the riches of God's grace that He lavished on us with all wisdom and understanding." (Ephesians 1:7, 8)

"Praise the Lord O my soul...who forgives all your sins." (Psalm 103:1, 3)

What if the minimum basic charge to stay in Heaven is one million dollars ($1,000,000) per day?

Not many of us could afford even the first few days in Heaven. Furthermore, the daily charge probably would get more expensive each day as God reveals more and more of His glory. Who could possibly pay for the first year in Heaven? And eternity continues for hundreds of thousands of billions of years--forever!

We Christians are so fortunate that God not only invites us to go to Heaven but also to stay there for free.

"$100,000,000,000,000,000,000,000,000,000,000 plus value" freely given by God when you accept Jesus Christ as Lord of your life and then He allows you to stay forever in Heaven. And that is just the beginning!

Who wouldn't be "filled with a glorious and inexpressible joy because we have achieved the goal of our faith, the salvation of our souls." (1Peter 1: 8, 9)

What a deal!

"Surely goodness and love will follow me all the days of my life, and I will dwell in the house of the LORD forever." (Psalm 23:6)

"Praise be to the God and Father of our Lord Jesus Christ, who has blessed us in the heavenly realms with every spiritual blessing in Christ." (Ephesians 1:3)

"But Stephen, full of the Holy Spirit, looked up to heaven and saw the glory of God, and Jesus standing at the right hand of God." (Acts 7:55)

"You will fill me with joy in your presence, with eternal pleasures at your right hand." (Psalm 16:11)

What if the Jesus that you normally visualize has now completely changed back into his former glory that he had before he came to earth?

Now He is no longer in a 170 pound body breathing air but rather He has returned into His former spiritual body! He has resumed His original beauty and magnificence. Although He is invisible to human eyes, He is clearly visible in the spiritual kingdom and He is all powerful, all knowing and everywhere present (omniscient and omnipresent).

In our prayer life we usually visualize Christ as the 170 pound suffering servant, but He has risen! He has resumed His former Godly attributes that He set aside when He came to earth.

Envision Him now as the Son of God in all of His former glory, wisdom and power. Note also that He will return shortly!

Christ left heaven and "made himself nothing, taking the very nature of a servant, being made in human likeness. And being found in appearance as a man, he humbled himself and became obedient to death— even death on a cross!" (Philippians 2:7-8)

"Father, I (Jesus) want those you have given me to be with me where I am, and to see my glory, the glory you have given me because you loved me before the creation of the world." (John 17:24)

"I saw heaven standing open and there before me was a white horse, whose rider is called Faithful and True. With justice he judges and makes war. His eyes are like blazing fire, and on his head are many crowns. He has a name written on him that no one knows but he himself. He is dressed in a robe dipped in blood, and his name is the Word of God. The armies of heaven were following him, riding on white horses and dressed in fine linen, white and clean. Out of his mouth comes a sharp sword with which to strike down the nations. "He will rule them with an iron scepter." He treads the winepress of the fury of the wrath of God Almighty. On his robe and on his thigh he has this name written: KING OF KINGS AND LORD OF LORDS."
(Revelation 19:11-16)

"Behold, I am coming soon! My reward is with me, and I will give to everyone according to what he has done. I am the Alpha and the Omega, the First and the Last, the Beginning and the End." (Revelation 22:12, 13)

What if you could have been Jesus' best friend in his grade school and into junior high?

He would have been so much fun to play with. He probably was daring and courageous, going where most would have been afraid to go. He visited with priests in the Temple and even taught them.

He was a model of moderation; no temper tantrums, no pity parties, no coarse jokes. He didn't get bent out of shape when maligned by others. He was very sensitive to hurting people. Jesus had awesome inner beauty!

Would you have been one of Christ's close friends if you were in His class? I wish I could have been. It would have been wonderful to have been Christ's best friend when He was young.

Unfortunately that is impossible, but each one of us can be Christ's best friend now! He is much more available now than if we had actually been His classmate. He never sleeps; and when I can't sleep, He is right beside me. I can be "closer than a brother" to Jesus; and I can be a "man after Christ's own heart"! I can. . .I can. . .I can!

<u>I CAN BE CHRIST'S BEST FRIEND AND HE CAN BE MY BEST FRIEND TODAY!</u>

"Come near to God and he will come near to you."
(James 4:8)

"Never will I leave you; never will I forsake you."
(Hebrews 13:5)

"To them God has chosen to make known among the
Gentiles the glorious riches of this mystery, which is
Christ in you, the hope of glory." (Colossians 1:27)

"I have been crucified with Christ and I no longer
live, but Christ lives in me. The life I live in the
body, I live by faith in the Son of God, who loved me
and gave himself for me." (Galatians 2:20)

"My prayer is not for them alone. I pray also for
those who will believe in me through their message,
that all of them may be one, Father, just as you are
in me and I am in you. May they also be in us so that
the world may believe that you have sent me. I have
given them the glory that you gave me, that they
may be one as we are one: I in them and you in me.
May they be brought to complete unity to let the
world know that you sent me and have loved them
even as you have loved me." (John 17:20-24)

What if God had planned for you to be the pivotal instrument in saving seven people during your lifetime!

Your life of witnessing, prayer, and Godly love had been scheduled to bring seven people into a personal relationship with Christ. Now, however, imagine that your life is over. Unfortunately only four of the seven have come to know Christ as their personal Savior!

Your life is reviewed in Heaven and it becomes evident that you were sidetracked by greed and jealousy, which prevented two of the people from seeing Jesus in you. Your apathy and laziness prevented another from becoming saved.

Although "salvation belongs to the Lord," God chooses to work through each one of us. We each have an awesome responsibility with a huge task that is bigger than each one of us. But "With God all things are possible!" (Matthew 19:26))

"When the disciples heard this, they were greatly astonished and asked, 'Who then can be saved?' Jesus looked at them and said, 'With man this is

impossible, but with God all things are possible.'"
(Matthew 19:23, 26)

"I tell you, open your eyes and look at the fields!
They are ripe for harvest. Even now the reaper
draws his wages, even now he harvests the crop for
eternal life, so that the sower and the reaper may
be glad together." (John 4:35,36)

"Jesus said to his disciples: 'Things that cause
people to sin are bound to come, but woe to that
person through whom they come. It would be better
for him to be thrown into the sea with a millstone
tied around his neck than for him to cause one of
these little ones to sin.'" (Luke 17:1, 2)

"The one who received the seed that fell among the
thorns is the man who hears the word, but the
worries of this life and the deceitfulness of wealth
choke it, making it unfruitful." (Matthew 13:22)

"Son of man, I have made you a watchman for the
house of Israel; so hear the word I speak and give
them warning from me. When I say to the wicked,
'O wicked man, you will surely die,' and you do not
speak out to dissuade him from his ways, that
wicked man will die for his sin, and I will hold you
accountable for his blood. But if you do warn the

wicked man to turn from his ways and he does not do so, he will die for his sin, but you will have saved yourself.'" (Ezekiel 33: 7-9)

What if God's hatred and disgust for our sin is far more revolting to Him than anything that we can imagine?

If we only knew how grievous our sin is to God, we would be very embarrassed, humiliated, and distressed. God loathes our sin and it grieves Him.

When we get to Heaven, we will be astonished at God's great love for us in light of how awful even our smallest sin saddened Him.

"Because of the Lord's great love we are not consumed, for his compassions never fail. They are new every morning; great is your faithfulness." (Lamentations 3:22, 23)

"I am the LORD your God; consecrate yourselves and be holy, because I am holy." (Leviticus 11:44)

"Be perfect, therefore, as your heavenly Father is perfect." (Matthew 5:48)

"As obedient children, do not conform to the evil desires you had when you lived in ignorance. But just as he who called you is holy, so be holy in all you do; for it is written: "Be holy, because I am holy." 1 Peter 1:14)

"Don't be fooled by those who try to excuse these sins, for the anger of God will fall on all who disobey him." (Ephesians 5:6)

"For the wages of sin is death, but the gift of God is eternal life in Christ Jesus our Lord." (Romans 6:23)

"Yet he was merciful; he forgave their iniquities and did not destroy them. Time after time he restrained his anger and did not stir up his full wrath." (Psalm 78:38)

"For God so loved the world that he gave his one and only Son, that whoever believes in him shall not perish but have eternal life." (John 3:16)

What if everything in this life is just a small glimpse of what eternal life in Heaven is really like?

Compared to our future life in Heaven, this earth life is like being an embryo in a mother's uterus. Little embryos can feel and hear and taste. But they really don't have a clue as to how spectacular life as an adult human will be!

Compared to actually living in Heaven, we are each now in the "embryo stage" of experiencing Heaven on earth. We really can't imagine how spectacular Heaven life will be. Even so, we do feel a bit of Heaven here on earth. We can taste and see a bit of Heaven in our lives. We can hear God's voice faintly, and we can see Him work.

This earthly embryo stage is almost nothing compared to experiencing God and His Glory in Heaven. From one little embryo to another, seek hard the Kingdom of Heaven. It is going to be awesome!

"However, as it is written: "No eye has seen, no ear has heard, no mind has conceived what God has prepared for those who love him." (1 Corinthians 2:9)

"Surely goodness and love will follow me all the days of my life, and I will dwell in the house of the LORD forever." (Psalm 23:9)

"You have made known to me the path of life; you will fill me with joy in your presence, with eternal pleasures at your right hand." (Psalm 16:11)

What if you were one additional teacher at Columbine when Eric and Dylan massacred 12 students and 1 teacher?

What if Dylan had you face down with the pistol touching the back of your head. He yells excitedly; "Are you a Christian?" You hesitate knowing that he hates Christians. He yells again; "Are you a Christian?"

We have one of two choices;

> #1. "Yes, I am a Christian." The pistol plummets us into eternity with Christ!
> OR
> #2. "No, I am not a Christian." We lie to live another day.

To our great dismay, Dylan yells, 'You coward! You renounced Christianity." The pistol fires, and we plummet into eternity but without Christ.

"Whoever acknowledges me before men, I will also acknowledge him before my Father in heaven. But whoever disowns me before men, I will disown him before my Father in heaven." (Matthew 10:32, 33)

"Who is the liar? It is the man who denies that Jesus is the Christ? Such a man is the antichrist— he denies the Father and the Son. No one who denies the Son has the Father; whoever acknowledges the Son has the Father also." (1 John 2:22, 23)

What if the birds are actually chirping a high level of praise to God?

We often think that birds are singing meaningless twitterings, but they probably are not doing anything meaningless. They sing during the early morning hours possibly thanking God for a new day. They very likely generate a high quality of praise that is difficult for us humans to achieve. At night, they twitter praise and thanksgiving before sleeping.

It is highly probable that God's creatures worship God in languages that we, at present, don't understand. If we could understand their communications, we would most likely be amazed to hear praise and worship to God in many new and wonderful ways.

God's animals might be doing a better job praising God than we humans do with our many distractions. We humans would do well to praise and thank our Creator much more than we do. Let's catch up!

"My mouth will speak in praise of the LORD. Let every creature praise his holy name for ever and ever." (Psalm 145:21)

"Let everything that has breath praise the LORD. Praise the LORD." (Psalm 150:6)

What if every sparrow that falls (dies) to the ground falls only by God's permission?

Scripture implies that God is in control of each sparrow's death! There are billions of sparrows on planet earth and they are able to live up to 20 years. Sparrows are possibly the most common and ordinary of all birds. Many other birds seem far more important. In spite of their huge numbers and lack of importance, God doesn't allow any to fall to the ground without His permission.

Why are you so worried about God's ability to love and care for you? God easily micro-manages the ordinary sparrows. How much more does He care for you! He knows everything that is happening to you and is working everything to work together for good in your life. He and He alone, cares about every small detail in your life. He will not allow anything to happen to you outside of His permissive will.

"Do not be afraid of those who kill the body but cannot kill the soul. Rather, be afraid of the One who can destroy both soul and body in hell. Are not two sparrows sold for a penny? Yet not one of them will fall to the ground apart from the will of your Father. And even the very hairs of your head are all numbered. So don't be afraid; you are worth more than many sparrows." (Matthew 10:28-31)

"For I know the plans I have for you," declares the Lord, "plans to prosper you and not to harm you, plans to give you hope and a future."   (Jeremiah 29:11)

"All things work together for good to those that love the Lord and are called according to His plan." (Romans 8:28)

"I am the Lord, the God of all mankind. Is anything too hard for me?" (Jeremiah 32:27)

What if your prayer has only the power of a slingshot?

What if your mom's prayer has the spiritual power of a 30:06 rifle? What if your Godly uncle prays with the power of a Howitzer cannon? God desires each of us to mature spiritually to the level of using a 45 MM tank cannon mounted on a turret with a revolving chair and motorized ammo feed!

Scripture tells us that "the prayer of the righteous is powerful and effective." Many Christians go into spiritual battles with slingshots when God desires them to be using powerful, effective prayer weapons.

Scripture talks of the "Sword of the Spirit" which was appropriate for two centuries ago. Now, the same Scripture would probably read "the machine gun of the Spirit!"

There are prayer nuclear bombs available! Don't be satisfied with the prayer power of a sling shot!

"The prayer of a righteous man is powerful and effective." (James 5:16)

"Elijah was a man just like us. He prayed earnestly that it would not rain, and it did not rain on the land for three and a half years. Again he prayed, and the heavens gave rain, and the earth produced its crops." (James 5:16-18)

"I tell you the truth, anyone who has faith in me will do what I have been doing. He will do even greater things than these, because I am going to the Father. And I will do whatever you ask in my name, so that the Son may bring glory to the Father. You may ask me for anything in my name, and I will do it." (John 14:12-14)

"If you remain in me and my words remain in you, ask whatever you wish, and it will be given you." (John 15:7)

"In the same way, the Spirit helps us in our weakness. We do not know what we ought to pray for, but the Spirit himself intercedes for us with groans that words cannot express." (Romans 8:26)

"And take the Helmet of Salvation, and the Sword of the Spirit which is the word of God. With all prayer and petition pray at all times in the Spirit..." (Ephesians 6:17, 18)

What if you could do something today that would make a difference for your entire time in eternity?

What if, when you put money in the church offering plate, it results in an eternal reward for yourself? Or what if you give a "cup of cold water" to someone in Jesus' name, it would change something, even if only slightly better, forever for yourself?

Much of what we do each day has no eternal significance. Our short-lived pleasures come and go and are soon forgotten. Lord, forgive us for the huge time wastage in our lives that is not useful for us or you--too much time spent with the TV, computer, or sleep, just to name few.

Nevertheless, there are countless opportunities each day that could be used to lay up treasure for eternity and most are very easy to do! There are endless variations of "cups of cold water" such as a timely smile or a word of encouragement. Consider that any activity of love toward God or your neighbor will result in an increased reward for you forever in Heaven.

"Do not store up for yourselves treasures on earth, where moth and rust destroy, and where thieves break in and steal. But store up for your selves treasures in heaven, where moth and rust do not destroy, and where thieves do not break in and steal. For where your treasure is, there your heart will be also." (Matthew 6:19-21)

"But when you fast, put oil on your head and wash your face, so that it will not be obvious to men that you are fasting, but only to your Father, who is unseen; and your Father, who sees what is done in secret, will reward you." (Matthew 6:17, 18)

"What is your life? You are a mist that appears for a little while and then vanishes. Instead, you ought to say, 'If it is the Lord's will, we will live and do this or that.' As it is, you boast and brag. All such boasting is evil. Anyone, then, who knows the good he ought to do and doesn't do it, sins." (James 4:14-17)

"Love your enemies! Then your reward from Heaven will be very great." (Luke 6:35)

"So do not throw away this confident trust in the Lord. Remember the great reward it brings you! Patient endurance is what you need now, so that you will continue to do God's will. Then you will receive all that he has promised." (Hebrews 10:35, 36)

What if, like in the game of Monopoly, God has a "fast track" to Heaven planned for some select people?

In Monopoly you can land on "Go Directly to Go" and therefore miss out on all the pitfalls to get there and also collect $200. Perhaps God, in His magnificent wisdom, allows some Christians to go directly to Heaven early and miss all the pitfalls of life that can cause pain and sorrow!

When this happens, the Christian person is the winner because he goes directly to Heaven. When this happens, God is the winner because He is looking forward to a closer relationship with the person which is not possible while the person is living on earth. The departed person and God are celebrating activities beyond our human imagination and they have no regrets, no sorrow, and no loss.

When death occurs, relatives and friends feel like the losers because they lose out on more good times together. Those left behind grieve and "pick up the pieces" adjusting to life without the departed person.

It is important to grieve well. However, part of grieving well is to accept God's wisdom when He allows some Christians to go on the "fast tract" to Heaven. We who are on the "slow tract" will get there soon enough because life really is just a quick "mist" even for the aged.

"Precious in the sight of the LORD is the death of his saints." **(Psalms 116:15))**

"What is your life? You are a mist that appears for a little while and then vanishes." (James 4:14)

"Do not let your hearts be troubled. Trust in God ; trust also in me. In my Father's house are many rooms; if it were not so, I would have told you. I am going there to prepare a place for you. And if I go and prepare a place for you, I will come back and take you to be with me that you also may be where I am. You know the way to the place where I am going." (John 14:1-4)

"You have made known to me the path of life; you will fill me with joy in your presence, with eternal pleasures at your right hand." (Psalm 16:11)

"Surely goodness and love will follow me all the days of my life and I will dwell in the house of the Lord forever." (Psalm 23:6)

What if God answered all our prayers immediately just as we prayed them?

There would be no need for hospitals, doctors, nurses, clinics, and medicine. All the people who prayed for wealth would be very rich and thus very few would ever work again. Restaurants, golf courses, and beaches would be packed.

Most people would pray to become healthy, wealthy, wise, and beautiful. But would God be treasured above all else? Would faith disappear since it would be an unnecessary relic from the past? Would God be loved more (or less) if He answered everyone's prayers immediately and completely?

God is so wise, and He always gives us the very best answers to our prayers. He answers them in the most loving and perfect way. We may not understand why He answers our individual prayers in the way that He does, but His ways are always the best.

His goal is to get us into Heaven as strong, spiritually fit warriors; not as lazy wimps. He accomplishes this goal in the most painless way possible with great wisdom and love. It is very good that God is so gentle and loving with us or our "education courses" preparing us for Heaven would be much more painful!

"Consider it pure joy, my brothers, whenever you face trials of many kinds, because you know that the testing of your faith develops perseverance. Perseverance must finish its work so that you may be mature and complete, not lacking anything."
(James 1:1-4)

"For our light and momentary troubles are achieving for us an eternal glory that far outweighs them all."
(2 Corinthians 4:17)

"I tell you the truth, anyone who has faith in me will do what I have been doing. He will do even greater things than these, because I am going to the Father. And I will do whatever you ask in my name, so that the Son may bring glory to the Father. You may ask me for anything in my name, and I will do it." (John 14:12-14)

"As for God, his way is perfect; the word of the Lord is flawless." (2 Samuel 22:31)

What if poverty is one of God's most valuable gifts that He gives to many of the people He loves?

Meager resources of wealth may be a wonderful gift from God beyond our imagination! On the other hand, extravagant wealth may be a terrible burden that actually makes it very difficult to get into Heaven. To have basic food, shelter, and clothing is all that we really need. With these three items present in our lives, we really lack nothing. <u>In fact, we may have more because we have less!</u>

To be content and satisfied with less sometimes results in our being rich with things that are really important. There may be more love and joy in our lives because we are helping each other. Poverty somehow encourages people to have faith in God for their needs instead of faith in themselves. Poverty promotes a healthy prayer life. Poverty often times produces a serious dependence on God.

Heaven may be heavily populated by people who have been poor during their lifetime. Poverty may be one of God's most wonderful gifts leading to a deeper walk with Him!

"The LORD sends poverty and wealth; he humbles and he exalts. He raises the poor from the dust and lifts the needy from the ash heap; he seats them with princes and has them inherit a throne of honor." (1 Samuel 2:7, 8)

"Delight yourself in the LORD and he will give you the desires of your heart. Commit your way to the LORD; trust in him and he will do this:" (Psalm 37:4, 5)

"And my God will meet all your needs according to his glorious riches in Christ Jesus." (Philippians 4:19)

"Then Jesus said to his disciples, 'I tell you the truth, it is hard for a rich man to enter the kingdom of heaven. Again I tell you, it is easier for a camel to go through the eye of a needle than for a rich man to enter the kingdom of God.'" (Matthew 19:23, 24)

What if our prayers never disappear but rather get turned into incense that is enjoyed forever in front of God's throne?

John writes in Revelation that "They (the 24 elders) were holding golden bowls full of incense, which are the prayers of the saints." (Revelation 5:8)

When we arrive in Heaven, we may be able to walk over to the golden bowls holding our prayers that have been collected by God from our earth life. We may smell each one of them as a pleasing aroma. Possibly we also will be able to see them, read them, and hear them over and over again if we wish. It will be very interesting to see how our prayers join with the prayers of the saints. All will appreciate the sweet smelling fragrance. This incense will be eternal and will be enjoyed forever in God's throne room.

Next time that you pray, visualize that your prayer goes directly into God's golden bowl in front of the throne. The prayer becomes wonderful, sweet incense of praise and enjoyment for God and all of God's people! Prayers may never disappear.

Lay up incense in Heaven. PRAY MORE. . .MUCH MORE!

"Each one (four living creatures and the twenty-four elders) had a harp and they were holding golden bowls full of incense, which are the prayers of the saints." (Revelation 5:8)

"O LORD, I call to you; come quickly to me. Hear my voice when I call to you. May my prayer be set before you like incense; may the lifting up of my hands be like the evening sacrifice." (Psalm 141:1,2)

"He, (another angel) was given much incense to offer, with the prayers of all the saints, on the golden altar before the throne. The smoke of the incense, together with the prayers of the saints, went up before God from the angel's hand." (Revelation 8:13)

"But thanks be to God, who always leads us in triumphal procession in Christ and through us spreads everywhere the fragrance of the knowledge of him, for we are to God the aroma of Christ among those who are being saved and those who are perishing." (12 Corinthians 2:14, 15)

"Be joyful always; pray continually; give thanks in all circumstances, for this is God's will for you in Christ Jesus." (1 Thessalonians 5:16)

"The prayer of a righteous man is powerful and effective." (James 5:16b)

What if we could enter into a bubble filled totally with God's love?

When inside God's love bubble, we would experience ever increasing cleansing with His wonderfully satisfying, exhilarating love. Stress, worry, and pain would be washed away, sometimes quickly but other times gradually.

Inside God's "love bubble," our sin and depression would begin to melt. Fear and anger would disappear. As we experience more and more of God's love in the bubble, there would flow from inside of us fresh levels of gratitude and contentment.

Our senses would awaken to feel thrills and delights that we didn't know existed prior to the love bubble. We would be free to explore God's grace and peace in a new level never experienced before.

Entrance into God's love bubble is through the door of faith! We Christians are so fortunate! Entrance is free and is always available. God is present there in a powerful way. Many people miss the love bubble because of distractions far less satisfying. Don't lose out. Enjoy being in God's love bubble as often as possible.

"God is love, and the one who abides in love abides in God, and God abides in him." "There is no fear in love' but perfect love casts out fear..." "We love because He first loved us." (1 John 4:16, 18, 19)

"Keep me safe, O God, for in you I take refuge." (Psalm 16:1)

"You have made known to me the path of life; you will fill me with joy in your presence, with eternal pleasures at your right hand." (Psalm 16:11)

"May the Lord make your love increase and overflow for each other and for everyone else, just as ours does for you. May he strengthen your hearts so that you will be blameless and holy in the presence of our God and Father when our Lord Jesus comes with all his holy ones." (1 Thessalonians 3:12, 13)

"In the shelter of your presence you hide them from the intrigues of men; in your dwelling you keep them safe from accusing tongues." (Psalm 31: 20)

"God will supply all your needs from His glorious riches, which have been given to us in Christ Jesus." (Philippians 4:19)

What if you make a huge "OOPS" out of your life?

The biggest "OOPS" is to have lived your entire life without God. "OOPS" can be corrected at any time during your lifetime but it makes no sense to wait too long. If you do, you will miss out on many benefits that God affords. Don't forget that it is impossible to correct the "OOPS" after death.

Don't miss Heaven for the world. To gain the whole world but lose your soul is the biggest "OOPS" possible!

"What good will it be for a man if he gains the whole world, yet forfeits his **soul**? Or what can a man give in exchange for his **soul**?" (Matthew 16:26)

"Now choose life, so that you and your children may live and that you may love the Lord your God, listen to his voice, and hold fast to Him. For the Lord is your life . . ." (Deuteronomy 30:19, 20)

"Choose for yourselves this day whom you will serve...But as for me and my household, we will serve the Lord." (Joshua 24:15)

What if there is absolutely no excuse good enough to present to God at the Judgment?

Many people are preparing a "hard question" to give to God when they see Him face to face after they die. Some people have lists of "difficult questions" which they feel will stump God. Most have the intent that if God can't answer their tough question, then they should not be held responsible for their own personal behavior.

I have tried to think up a really tough question that God will not be able to answer. I can't think of even one that would come close. Do you know of any tough questions?

There is "the trilemma": (God is all loving; God is all powerful; Pain and suffering exist.) but God has an easy answer for that question.

At some point give up trying to find the really tough question. It is impossible to stump God! Rather align yourself perfectly with the will of the Judge. There is no excuse trying to find a good excuse. It is just not going to be found.

"For my thoughts are not your thoughts, neither are your ways my ways," declares the LORD. "As the heavens are higher than the earth, so are my ways higher than your ways and my thoughts than your thoughts." (Isaiah 55:8, 9)

"But God made the earth by his power; he founded the world by his wisdom and stretched out the heavens by his understanding. When he thunders, the waters in the heavens roar; he makes clouds rise from the ends of the earth. He sends lightning with the rain and brings out the wind from his storehouses." (Jeremiah 51:15, 16)

"Oh, the depth of the riches of the wisdom and knowledge of God! How unsearchable his judgments, and his paths beyond tracing out! 'Who has known the mind of the Lord? Or who has been his counselor?' 'Who has ever given to God, that God should repay him?' For from him and through him and to him are all things. To him be the glory forever! Amen." (Romans 11:33-36)

"When times are good, be happy; but when times are bad, consider; God has made the one as well as the other." (Ecclesiastes 7:14)

What if eternity is measured by an eagle flying to the ocean and picking up one grain of sand every 100 years?

The eagle flies to a big desert and drops it. When that pile of sand, dropped one grain at a time every 100 years finally becomes bigger in mass than Mount Everest, eternity has just begun.

Imagine that the eagle continues every hundred years dropping a grain of sand on top of this Mount Everest if it could. After an eternity, it seems, the dropping spot will enlarge to become same size as planet earth. Even after all that time that has passed, eternity has just only begun!

Invest in eternal values with all your strength. Or to say it in another way, "Love the Lord your God with all your heart, soul, strength, and mind. And love your neighbor as well."

Lay up treasure in Heaven because eternity in Heaven lasts a very long time! Time goes at the same "speed" in Hell, it is just that it seems so much longer than time spent in Heaven.

"Praise be to you, O LORD, God of our father Israel, from everlasting to everlasting." (1 Chronicles 29:10)

"And the Levites...said: 'Stand up and praise the LORD your God, who is from everlasting to everlasting." (Nehemiah 9:5)

"At the end of that time, I, Nebuchadnezzar, raised my eyes toward heaven, and my sanity was restored. Then I praised the Most High; I honored and glorified him who lives forever. His dominion is an eternal dominion; his kingdom endures from generation to generation." (Daniel 4:34)

"Now a man came up to Jesus and asked, 'Teacher, what good thing must I do to get eternal life?'... If you want to enter life, obey the commandments.'" (Matthew 19:17)

"Then he will say to those on his left, 'Depart from me, you who are cursed, into the eternal fire prepared for the devil and his angels. For I was hungry and you gave me nothing to eat, I was thirsty and you gave me nothing to drink, I was a stranger and you did not invite me in, I needed clothes and you did not clothe me, I was sick and in prison and you did not look after me.'

They also will answer, 'Lord, when did we see you hungry or thirsty or a stranger or needing clothes or

sick or in prison, and did not help you?' He will
reply, 'I tell you the truth, whatever you did not do
for one of the least of these, you did not do for me.'
Then they will go away to eternal punishment, but
the righteous to eternal life." (Matthew 25:16-46)

What if salvation is like a pregnancy?

A pregnancy may start small but smallness doesn't really matter regarding pregnancy. Either one is totally pregnant or not pregnant at all.

Just as it is impossible to be half alive or half pregnant, in similar fashion, people are either saved or not saved. They are either totally Christian or not Christian at all. Why do so many people assume that they can be partial Christians?

Many people consider themselves pretty much saved! They are pretty good and in the balance of goodness and badness, the scale should tip to the goodness side. Can you imagine a person being three-fourths saved? For eternity, three-fourths of the person lives in heaven and the other one fourth lives in hell.

Praise God that He saves us completely. We are totally saved when we accept Christ as our personal Savior.

"No one can serve two masters. Either he will hate the one and love the other, or he will be devoted to the one and despise the other. You cannot serve both God and money." (Matthew 6:24)

"Then we will no longer be infants, tossed back and forth by the waves, and blown here and there by every wind of teaching and by the cunning and craftiness of men in their deceitful scheming. Instead, speaking the truth in love, we will in all things grow up into him who is the Head, that is, Christ."(Ephesians 4:14, 15)

"Not everyone who says to me, 'Lord, Lord,' will enter the kingdom of heaven, but only he who does the will of my Father who is in heaven." (Matthew 7:21)

"I know your deeds, that you are neither cold nor hot. I wish you were either one of the other! So, because you are lukewarm--neither hot nor cold--I am about to spit you out of my mouth." (Revelations 3:16)

"Teacher, which is the greatest commandment in the Law?" Jesus replied: "Love the Lord your God with all your heart and with all your soul and with all your mind.' This is the first and greatest commandment." (Matthew 22:36-37)

What if my dog or cat gets a better grade than I get?

What if my dog or cat shows more love for me, it's master, than I show to my Master in Heaven? Sometimes pets are better lovers than we humans are. Dogs are so excited to see their masters come home. They bark and jump and wave their tails. Cats meow and wind their body and tail around our ankles. Pets are really exceptional at showing love to their masters. My pet might do a better job loving me than I do loving God!

God has given us so much. He is a wonderful master. He provides us with special abilities and life's experiences sent specifically for our pleasure. He sends the Holy Spirit to guide us through life. He comforts us in trouble. He trains us by sending us to his "Special Obedience School." He puts each of us "to sleep" when it is time to stop living and to come home to heaven. God loves us so much. We are made to love him back.

What a shame if my dog or cat gets a better mark than I do in loving the Master? Always love God much more than your dog or cat loves you!

Love the Lord your God with all your heart and all your mind and all your strength and all your soul. (Matthew 23:47) (Deuteronomy 6:5)

"The Lord your God is testing you to find out whether you love him with all your heart and with all your soul." (Deuteronomy 13:3)

"So be very careful to love the LORD your God." (Joshua 23:11)

"Again Jesus said, 'Simon son of John, do you truly love me?' He answered, 'Yes, Lord, you know that I love you.' Jesus said, 'Take care of my sheep.' "(John 21:16)

"If I give all I possess to the poor and surrender my body to the flames, but have not love, I gain nothing. Love is patient, love is kind. It does not envy, it does not boast, it is not proud. It is not rude, it is not self-seeking, it is not easily angered, it keeps no record of wrongs. Love does not delight in evil but rejoices with the truth. It always protects, always trusts, always hopes, always perseveres. Love never fails." (1 Corinthians 13:3-8)

"But the fruit of the Spirit is love, joy, peace, patience, kindness, goodness, faithfulness, gentleness and self-control." (Galatians 5:22)

"Whoever has my commands and obeys them, he is the one who loves me. He who loves me will be loved by my Father, and I too will love him and show myself to him." (John 14:21)

What if we experienced one minute of life in heaven--just 60 seconds of spectacular, glorious, awesome, incredible Heaven!

The spectacular sounds and tastes and colors would amaze us. But that is nothing compared to being in the presence of our awesome Creator God. To experience God would be a far more wonderful and thrilling than anything that we can imagine!

After that 60-second experience, could we return to working the usual 40-hour week? Could we return to the laundry, changing diapers, and sweeping up after others? Could we go back to sleepless nights and the mundane challenges of life?

NO!

Lord, don't let us know so much about Heaven that we would rather die than live one more moment here on earth!

"No eye has seen, no ear has heard, no mind has conceived what God has prepared for those who love him." (1 Corinthians 2:7)

In my Father's house are many rooms...I, Jesus, go to prepare a place for you. . .I will come back and take you to be with me that you also may be where I am. (John 14:1,3)

"Surely goodness and love will follow me all the days of my life, and I will dwell in the house of the LORD forever." (Psalms 23:6)

"You have made known to me the path of life; you will fill me with joy in your presence, with eternal **pleasures** at your right hand." (Psalm 16:11)

What if God charged a penalty to obtain forgiveness?

The following is an average suggested penalty depending on the seriousness of the sin:

One hour of heavy physical work to get one "minor" sin forgiven.

One week working in a coal mine without breaks for "moderate level" sin.

20 years cleaning prison toilets for taking the Lord's Name in vain, cursing God when frustrated or any other form of treason.

There is no forgiveness for blaspheming the Holy Spirit!

Imagine the work-related penalties that some people accumulate in a life time! Always be very, very grateful for the forgiveness that Jesus has provided for us so that we can escape the penalty of sin!

If we confess our sins, God is just and will forgive our sins and cleanse us from all unrighteousness. (1John 1:9)

"as far as the east is from the west, so far has he removed our transgressions from us." (Psalm 103:12)

"Come now, let us reason together," says the LORD. "Though your sins are like scarlet, they shall be as white as snow; though they are red as crimson, they shall be like wool." **(Isaiah 1:18)**

"Forgive us our debts, as we also have forgiven our debtors. . .For if you forgive men when they sin against you, your heavenly Father will also forgive you. But if you do not forgive men their sins, your Father will not forgive your sins." (Matthew 6:12-15)

What if the Lord would remove the "BIG 3" from me?

PRIDE
GREED
LAZINESS

If these three were totally removed from me, what would be left? Would there be enough left so that people could recognize who I am?

It is my hope that after all pride, greed, and laziness are removed from me, there will still be enough love, faith, and good works for people to say, "Hello! I know you!"

It is so easy to become a bundle of prideful accumulations, one-upmanship, and self promotion. The Bible states that we will be tested in fire and all "hay, wood, and stubble will be burned up." After the fire cleansing, what will be left of me?

Make sure you will be recognized in Heaven at least by your love for God and your love for your neighbor!

"For no one can lay any foundation other than the one already laid, which is Jesus Christ. If any man builds on this foundation using gold, silver, costly stones, wood, hay or straw, his work will be shown for what it is, because the Day will bring it to light. It will be revealed with fire, and the fire will test the quality of each man's work. If what he has built survives, he will receive his reward. If it is burned up, he will suffer loss; he himself will be saved, but only as one escaping through the flames." (1 Corinthians 3:11-15)

"For we are God's workmanship, created in Christ Jesus to do good works, which God prepared in advance for us to do." (Ephesians 2:10)

"Love the Lord your God with all your heart and with all your soul and with all your mind. This is the first and greatest commandment. And the second is like it: Love your neighbor as yourself." (Matthew 22:37)

What if Satan has many different types of flaming arrows, but he prefers to use his five favorites the most?

Here are Satan's favorite five arrow picks that he uses most often:

1. Bitter "anger against God" or "anger against people" arrows.
2. White hot pride arrows.
3. Cold blue arrow of apathy and procrastination.
4. Sharp razor tipped $$$$$, power and fame distracter arrows.
5. Surprisingly high velocity "early death" arrow.

How he uses these top five arrow choices varies from individual to individual. All are released at full draw for maximum impact. Which of these five arrows would be most effective against you?

All of Satan's arrows have surprising accuracy to those people not wearing spiritual armor. Some are meant to wound and fester; others are lethal. BUT…they are perfectly harmless when used against the Shield of Faith and when the Word of God is protecting Christians against heart shots.

Put on the armor of God: The Helmet of salvation, the Breastplate of Righteousness, the Belt of Truth, the Feet that spread the Good News, the Sword of the Spirit and the Shield of Faith. (Ephesians 6)

"In addition to all this, take up the shield of faith, with which you can extinguish all the flaming arrows of the evil one." (Ephesians 6:16)

"Be self-controlled and alert. Your enemy the devil prowls around like a roaring lion looking for someone to devour. Resist him, standing firm in the faith. . ." (1 Peter 5:8,9)

"Hear me, O God, as I voice my complaint; protect my life from the threat of the enemy. Hide me from the conspiracy of the wicked, from that noisy crowd of evildoers. They sharpen their tongues like swords and aim their words like deadly arrows. They shoot from ambush at the innocent man; they shoot at him suddenly, without fear." (Psalm 64:1-4)

"He who dwells in the shelter of the Most High will rest in the shadow of the Almighty. . .You will not fear the terror of night, nor the arrow that flies by day," (Psalm 91:1,5)

What if I've been really busy and unable to do my devotions yesterday and today?

God will understand, I'm sure. I have been really busy. Of course, I did eat 3 meals yesterday; I'm not too busy for that. Then there was the news on TV, and I had a little relaxation here and there, but it has been busier than usual.

What if God were 1 or 2 days late answering my prayers once in a while just like I am 1 or 2 days late in my devotions with Him? He is busy too, you know. If God were occasionally late with us like we are occasionally late with Him, we would each probably be in big trouble.

God never uses the "too busy" excuse. Is that a good excuse for us to use with Him?
NO!

"indeed, he who watches over Israel will neither slumber nor sleep. . .the LORD will watch over your coming and going both now and forevermore." (Psalm 121:4, 8)

"Keep your lives free from the love of money and be content with what you have, because God has said, 'Never will I leave you; never will I **forsake** you.' "(Deuteronomy 31:6) (Hebrews 13:5)

"She had a sister called Mary, who sat at the Lord's feet listening to what he said. But Martha was distracted by all the preparations that had to be made. . .'Martha, Martha,' the lord answered, 'you are worried and upset about many things, but only one thing is needed. Mary has chosen what is better and it will not be taken away from her.' " (Luke 10:39-42).

What if God made me to be a snake instead of a human?

What if He had made me into a worm? What if He made me into an irritating fly or mosquito?

Praise God that He made me into a PERSON. . .a CHILD OF GOD!

So don't play the role of an irritating fly or mosquito. Don't be a cowardly worm; and, for Heaven's sake and more importantly, for your own sake, don't be an evil snake in the grass!

I don't understand why so many people want to be a fly or a worm or a snake.

BE A HUMAN FOR YOUR SAKE!

"Then God said, 'Let us make man in our image, in our likeness, and let them rule over the fish of the sea and the birds of the air, over the livestock, over all the earth, and over all the creatures that move along the ground.' So God created man in his own image, in the image of God he created him; male and female he created them." (Genesis 1:26, 27)

"Have I not commanded you? Be strong and courageous. Do not be terrified; do not be discouraged, for the LORD your God will be with you wherever you go." (Joshua 1:9)

"Be strong in the Lord and in His mighty power." (Ephesians 6:10)

"You made him ruler over the works of your hands; you put everything under his feet: all flocks and herds, and the beasts of the field, the birds of the air, and the fish of the sea, all that swim the paths of the seas. O Lord, our Lord, how majestic is your name in all the earth!" (Psalm 8:6-9)

What if God uses the "intermittent, irregular reward system" for answering our prayers in order to increase our faith and endurance?

Fishing, golfing, and gambling all use the same "intermittent, irregular reward system." In psychological experiments when using mice or monkeys, one can get the most pulls on the lever (work) for the least amount of food (reward) with this particular reward system.

God is in the wonderful business of increasing our faith and endurance. He always answers each prayer wisely and perfectly! God does not use the intermittent reward system to answer our prayers, but He may need to delay answering what we pray for so that we grow deeper with Him.

Praise God that He loves us so much! If you feel that your prayers are being answered in a random intermittent way, don't worry. God doesn't answer prayer randomly to grow your faith. He knows exactly what He is doing, and He answers each prayer in the wisest manner for our good.

"Be still before the LORD and wait patiently for him; (Psalm 37:7)

"Consider it pure joy, my brothers, whenever you face trials of many kinds, because you know that the testing of your faith develops perseverance. Perseverance must finish its work so that you may be mature and complete, not lacking anything." (James 1:2-4)

"Ask and it will be given to you; seek and you will find; knock and the door will be opened to you. For everyone who asks receives; he who seeks finds; and to him who knocks, the door will be opened." (Matthew 7:7,8)

"Which of you fathers, if your son asks for a fish, will give him a snake instead? Or if he asks for an egg, will give him a scorpion? If you then, though you are evil, know how to give good gifts to your children, how much more will your Father in heaven give the Holy Spirit to those who ask him!" (Luke 11, 9-11)

What if the life of sin and absence from God was so comfy and delicious and thrilling and tasty and restful and playful and glitzy and full of laughter and reckless abandon and happy, happy, happy... BUT... that life ended in eternal Hell?

After all that pleasure, eventually there will be death. Then each is ushered into the throne room of God. After amazement of how awesome God is, all will drop down and "bow the knee and confess that Jesus is Lord." A brief judgment service follows where the Book of Life is opened.

It is very important to have one's name written in the Book of Life. Those in the Book will be "filled with a glorious and inexpressible joy because they have achieved the goal of their faith, the salvation of their souls." (1Peter 1:8,9)

What a bad idea it is to miss out on eternal pleasure and joy with the Lord forever for a mere 70 to 100 years of glitz on earth? It is amazing that many people choose 70 years of "Godless pleasure" and risk losing "glorious and inexpressible joy" for eternity. Life on earth is so short and eternal life is so long!

CHOOSE WELL: Short-term glitz or inexpressible joy for eternity--it is such an easy decision!

"What is your life? You are a mist that appears for a little while and then vanishes." (James 4:14)

"What good is it for a man to gain the whole world, and yet lose or forfeit his very self?" (Luke 9:25)

"Enter through the narrow gate. For wide is the gate and broad is the road that leads to destruction, and many enter through it. But small is the gate and narrow the road that leads to life, and only a few find it." (Matthew 7:13, 14)

"No servant can serve two masters. Either he will hate the one and love the other, or he will be devoted to the one and despise the other. You cannot serve both God and money." (Luke 16:13)

What if Heaven is the "Great Equalizer"?

It is so easy for the Creator of the universe to equalize injustices, shortened lives, or any other inequalities experienced during life on earth. Heaven is the Great Equalizer! In Heaven any losses suffered for the Kingdom of God can be easily made right by special closeness to the Lord and His many blessings.

If you have experienced much more than your share of difficulties, persecution, depression, or whatever, take heart! In Heaven, God will easily make all difficulties that you have experienced more than worthwhile for you.

God is very fair and very just. Never forget; "HEAVEN IS THE GREAT EQUALIZER!"

"For our light and momentary suffering are working for us to achieve an eternal reward that far outweighs our suffering." (2 Corinthians 4:17)

"All things work together for good for those who love the Lord and are called according to His promise." (Romans 8:28)

"Rejoice and be glad because great is your reward in Heaven. . ." Matthew 5:12).

"However, as it is written: "No eye has seen, no ear has heard, no mind has conceived what God has prepared for those who love him"—(1 Corinthians 2:9)

"Blessed are you when people insult you, persecute you, and falsely say all kinds of evil against you because of me. Rejoice and be glad, because great is your reward in heaven. . ." (Matthew 5:11, 12)

"In this you greatly rejoice, though now for a little while you may have had to suffer grief in all kinds of trials. These have come so that your faith--of greater worth than gold, which perishes even though refined by fire—may be proved genuine and may result in praise, glory, and honor when Jesus Christ is revealed." (1 Peter:1:6, 7)

"Dear friends, do not be surprised at the painful trial you are suffering, as though something strange were happening to you. But rejoice that you participate in the sufferings of Christ, so that you may be overjoyed when his glory is revealed." (1 Peter 4:12,13)

What if there are three basic locations in Heaven for Christians to stay?

The first location is absolutely beautiful with beautiful rolling hills and valleys. The dwellings there are perfect and the meadows are filled with flowers. The deer browse and drink from the little stream rippling gently downhill.

The second location is lakeshore property and is absolutely gorgeous. It is a bit better than the first location. The meadows and flowers are spectacular and the deer and butterflies are fantastic. In addition, the lake makes it a fantastic, beautiful place with beach, swimming, and fishing.

The third location is absolutely spectacular and unbelievable of the highest order. It affords a spectacular ocean view from its amazing luxurious rooms. The meadows down to the ocean beach are breathtaking with deer and much more. Adventure on the ocean is easily available resulting in serious praise. This location is the best of all.

Christians entering Heaven will be living in one of the three locations and each location is totally heavenly. Christians living in any particular location will experience no pride or greed or envy. What if the basic location for each Christian is determined by his or her prayer life on planet earth!

How is your personal prayer life doing?

Author's note----Although one's prayer life on earth probably doesn't determine one's location in Heaven, the Bible does encourage maximizing your prayer life so that wonderful things can happen through you!

"The LORD detests the sacrifice of the wicked, but the prayer of the upright pleases him." (Proverbs 15:8)

"Never be lacking in zeal, but keep your spiritual fervor, serving the Lord. Be joyful in hope, patient in affliction, faithful in prayer." (Romans 12:11, 12)

"Devote yourselves to prayer, being watchful and thankful." (Colossians 4:2)

"And pray in the Spirit on all occasions with all kinds of prayers and requests. With this in mind, be alert and always keep on praying for all the saints." (Ephesians 6:18)

"Do not be anxious about anything, but in everything, by prayer and petition, with thanksgiving, present your requests to God." (Philippians 4:6)

"Be joyful always; pray continually; give thanks in all circumstances, for this is God's will for you in Christ Jesus." (1 Thessalonians 5:16-18)

"If you remain in me and my Word remains in you, ask whatever you wish and it will be given you." (John 15:7)

"Rejoice and be glad for great is your reward in heaven. . . (Matthew 5:12)

What if all sin were stinky, slimy, and a greenish brownish color?

Imagine also that sin is surrounded with mold around the edges and is repulsive to look at or touch. We would all be sinless!

Sin actually has all of the above yucky properties. In fact, it is really much more ugly and repulsive than the description above. It is just that all that ugliness is covered with dazzling gold and bright spots of thrill and easy happiness. The fragrance over all that stench is wonderful-- like fresh baked apple pie or fresh brewed coffee. Satan hides the ugliness and stench with special wrappings to trick us.

We live in a dangerous temptation-filled world. Flee from luscious sin like it's the plague! All sin sooner or later hurts much more than the pleasure derived from it. Sin is ugly and deadly even if it is wrapped in a package that you just can't resist!

"And lead us not into temptation, but deliver us from the evil one." (Matthew 6:13)

"Be self-controlled and alert. Your enemy the devil prowls around like a roaring lion looking for someone to devour. Resist him, standing firm in the faith, because you know that your brothers throughout the world are undergoing the same kind of sufferings." (1 Peter 5:8, 9)

"He (devil) was a murderer from the beginning, not holding to the truth, for there is no truth in him. When he **lies**, he speaks his native language, for he is a liar and the **father** of **lies**." (John 8:44)

What if every trouble that we experience is sent to us directly from God and meant for our good?

Could it possibly be that each problem we experience is allowed by God specifically for our good? The dosage, intensity, and timing of our difficulties are within His perfect will to grow and strengthen us. Some problems are allowed to develop patience; others are used to make us humble. Others bring us to our knees so that we can be big in the Kingdom of God. Eventually all problems are designed to develop us into obedient and faithful lovers of God.

"You intended it to harm me, but God intended it for good to accomplish what is now being done, the saving of many lives." (Genesis 50:20)

"I bring prosperity and create disaster; I the Lord, do all these things." (Isaiah 45:7)

"You (God) have put me in the lowest pit, in the darkest depths. Your wrath lies heavily upon me; you have overwhelmed me with all your waves." (Psalm 88:6)

"Though He (God) slay me, yet will I hope in Him. . ." (Job 13:15)

"Your plans for me are for my welfare and good, not to harm me." (Jeremiah 29:11)

"All things work together for good to those who love the Lord and are called according to His purpose." (Romans 8:28).

"So then, those who suffer according to God's will should commit themselves to their faithful Creator and continue to do good." (1 Peter 4:19)

"When times are good, be happy; but when times are bad, consider: God has made the one as well as the other." (Ecclesiastes 7:14)

What if God would encapsulate His love into a pill?

Once swallowed, Godly love would change how everything is seen. For instance, enemies would be seen as people made in the image of God and whom God loves dearly.

In spite of how the enemy has hurt you in the past, you now have a Godly compassion and respect for him. You simply swallowed God's love pill and looked his way. Now you see him as God sees him!

God, the Great Physician, prescribes 'Love Capsules' for us to swallow often. They are available by God's grace only. Listen to Him. He'll give one to you and help you know when to swallow it!

But I tell you: Love your enemies and pray for those who persecute you that you may be sons of your Father in Heaven. He causes his sun to rise on the evil and the good, and sends rain on the righteous and the unrighteous. If you love those who love you, what reward will you get?...Be perfect, therefore, as your heavenly Father is perfect. (Matthew 5: 44-48)

168

"Bless those who persecute you; bless and do not curse." (Romans 12:14)

"You, my brothers, were called to be free. But do not use your freedom to indulge the sinful nature; rather, serve one another in love. The entire law is summed up in a single command: 'Love your neighbor as yourself.' If you keep on biting and devouring each other, watch out or you will be destroyed by each other." (Galatians 5:13-15)

"Do not repay anyone evil for evil. Be careful to do what is right in the eyes of everybody. If it is possible, as far as it depends on you, live at peace with everyone. Do not take revenge, my friends, but leave room for God's wrath, for it is written: 'It is mine to avenge; I will repay,' says the Lord. 'On the contrary: If your enemy is hungry, feed him; if he is thirsty, give him something to drink.

In doing this, you will heap burning coals on his head. Do not be overcome by evil, but overcome evil with good." (Romans 12:17-21)

What if the joy of our salvation could be clarified better for us?

Sometimes we take our salvation for granted and we miss out on what an enormous value our salvation entails. We are so easily distracted with things of so little significance. Yet our incredibly valuable salvation goes unnoticed throughout many of our ordinary days.

St. Peter had it right when he stated that "we have this glorious and inexpressible joy because we have achieved the goal of our faith, the salvation of our souls." (1 Peter 1:8,9) If you are a Christian, where is your glorious, inexpressible joy?

The joy of our salvation is far greater than anything Prozac can do for us. The joy is greater than the lottery seems to promise. It is far more than success in business offers.

Collect a life time of pleasure from love, fame, wealth, and power and put them all onto one side of a weighing scale. Then put "the glorious and inexpressible joy because we've achieved the joy of our salvation" on the other side of the scale. The joy of our salvation is far weightier than anything else that life offers! There is no comparison between the value of our salvation compared to life's fleeting earthly pleasures.

If you are depressed, grumpy, helpless, and hopeless, just remember the trump card that Christians have in their spiritual pocket--the joy of their salvation! Perhaps we don't realize to the full measure, the great significance of our salvation but sooner or later we will in full.

"Though you have not seen Him, you love Him; and even though you do not see Him now, you believe in Him and are filled with an inexpressible and glorious joy, for you are receiving the goal of your faith, the salvation of your souls." (1 Peter 1:8/9)

Now we see but a poor reflection as in a mirror; then we shall see face to face. Now I know in part; then I shall know fully, even as I am fully known. (1 Corinthians 13:12)

You have made known to me the path of life; you will fill me with joy in your presence, with eternal **pleasures** at your right hand. (Psalm 16:11)

What if our total grade in life was the amount of Godly love we generated?

Godly love is defined as love toward God and love toward "our neighbor."

So often we think that our significance in life is related to the wealth, fame, or power that we accumulate. These actually are meaningless except in how they can be used in expressing Godly love.

It may be that the only valuable items in life are our love for God and our love for others!   All else is "hay, wood, and stubble" and gets burned up quickly.

After death, our "life grade" may be the total sum of our "Godly love level." An "A" is the best grade; however, many receive "Cs and Ds." What do you think your grade will be? Will it be an A, B, C, or D?

GOD IS LOVE and He commands us to love Him and love our neighbor. (Matthew 22:37)   That is our simple job description while on planet earth. We will each be graded on our "love level."

"The Lord your God is testing you to find out whether you love Him with all your heart and with all your soul. It is the Lord your God you must follow, and Him you must revere. Keep His commands and obey Him, serve Him and hold fast to Him." (Deuteronomy 13:3, 4)

"Test me, O LORD, and try me, examine my heart and my mind; for your love is ever before me, and I walk continually in your truth." (Psalm 26:2)

"Examine yourselves to see whether you are in the faith; test yourselves. Do you not realize that Christ Jesus is in you—unless, of course, you fail the test?" (2 Corinthians 13:5)

"Jesus replied: 'Love the Lord your God with all your heart and with all your soul and with all your mind.' This is the first and greatest commandment. And the second is like it: 'Love your neighbor as yourself.' " (Matthew 22:37-39)

What if the Seal, Bowl, and Trumpet judgments of Revelation could be accomplished now without God even using His power to make them happen?

It seems that, at present, we human beings have the nuclear and biological capabilities to accomplish all of those horrendous, cataclysmic events that the Bible portrays in Revelation, the last book of the Bible. All that is needed is a quick inflammatory catalyst to light the explosive events to begin God's divine "end-time program."

I suspect that we all should be ready to meet the Lord face to face at any time since we can't know exactly when the "end times" will arrive. Here are 4 tips for preparation for the Seal, Bowl, and Trumpet Judgments:

1. Be seriously saved. (Romans 10:9/10)
2. Forgive and get forgiven regarding any unresolved areas of conflict. (1 John 1:9)
3. Tell as many as possible around you how to get saved and do it now, starting with your closest family members, then neighbors and move outwards from there.

4. Make a difference for your eternity. Maximize your "good works" by giving, sharing, loving to the maximum until you are unable to do any more.

"That if you confess with your mouth, "Jesus is Lord," and believe in your heart that God raised him from the dead, you will be saved. For it is with your heart that you believe and are justified, and it is with your mouth that you confess and are saved." (Romans 10:9, 10)

"If we confess our sins, he is faithful and just and will forgive us our sins and purify us from all unrighteousness." (1 John 1:9)

"Forgive us our debts, as we also have forgiven our debtors." (Matthew 6:12)

"They replied, 'Believe in the Lord Jesus, and you will be saved—you and your household.' Then they spoke the word of the Lord to him and to all the others in his house." (Acts 16:31)

"Do not store up for yourselves treasures on earth, where moth and rust destroy, and where thieves break in and steal. But store up for your selves treasures in heaven, where moth and rust do not destroy, and where thieves do not break in and steal." (Matthew 6:19, 20)

"Behold I am coming soon! My reward is with me, and I will give to everyone according to what he has done. I am the Alpha and the Omega, the First and the Last, the Beginning and the End." (Revelation 22:12, 13)

"For as the lightning comes from the east and flashes to the west, so will be the coming of the Son of Man." (Matthew 24:27)

Why would God want to count and number the hair on everybody's head?

There are nearly 7 billion people alive on earth at present. Each person averages 100,000 hair per person (2,200 hairs per square inch) and God has them all numbered! That makes many trillions of possibilities for 1 hair to be actually that particular numbered hair.

Are you worried about God's ability to love and care for you? If He has the hair on your head counted and numbered, He must love you very much! He alone cares about every amazingly small detail in your life. Being that concerned about your hair, He must be much more concerned about the more important things in your life! Put your trust in God.

"Do not be afraid of those who kill the body but cannot kill the soul. Rather, be afraid of the One who can destroy both soul and body in hell. Are not two sparrows sold for a penny? Yet not one of them will fall to the ground apart from the will of your Father. And even the very hairs of your head are all numbered. So don't be afraid; you are worth more than many sparrows." (Matthew 10:28)[4]

"He determines the number of the stars and calls them each by name. Great is our Lord and mighty in power; his understanding has no limit." (Psalm 147:4,5)

"Oh, the depth of the riches of the wisdom and knowledge of God! How unsearchable his judgments, and his paths beyond tracing out!" (Romans 11:33)

"But God made the earth by his power; he founded the world by his wisdom and stretched out the heavens by his understanding." (Jeremiah 10:12)

"All things work together for good to those that love the Lord and are called according to His plan." Romans 8:28.

"Trust in the Lord with all your strength, lean not on your own understanding. In all your ways acknowledge Him and He will direct your path" (Proverbs 3: 5, 6)

What if I just had been assigned the awful task of cleaning and digging out the cabin outhouse pit?

The messy job would entail removing years of yucky, stinky, awful stuff that no one in their right mind would ever want to touch.

Jesus has offered to clean out each of our personal outhouses! It also is a stinky, yucky, painful, and pitiful job. To do it right, it cost Christ everything including His life.

What great love the Creator of the Universe, Jesus Christ, must have for each one of us because He personally has cleaned out each of our outhouses! He did it on the Cross willingly and out of love for us. No greater love has anyone than this, to die to remove our awful, stinky sin!

Have mercy on me, O God, according to your unfailing love; according to your great compassion blot out my transgressions. Wash away all my iniquity and cleanse me from my sin. For I know my transgressions, and my sin is always before me.

Against you, you only, have I sinned and done what is evil in your sight. . .Create in me a pure heart, O God and renew a steadfast spirit within me. (Psalm 51:1-4, 10)

"And being in anguish, he prayed more earnestly, and his sweat was like drops of blood falling to the ground."] (Luke 22:44)

"For the joy set before Him, Jesus endured the cross, disregarding its shame". (Hebrews 12:2)

"But God demonstrates his own love for us in this: While we were still sinners, Christ died for us." (Romans 5:8)

What if the agenda for the second day in Heaven looks like this?

1. Go to the edge of creation flying at the speed of thought. See all of creation in order to put things in perspective.

2. Breakfast with Jesus and the major Bible characters. Everybody whose names are written in the Book of Life are all major characters. No one is "lesser" in the Kingdom.

3. "Explore-and-touch" time. There are so many rooms and exciting places in the mansion prepared by God. Becoming distracted by exploring, touching, and visiting is never a problem. Time is never a limitation in Heaven.

4. Soap is not needed for sweat, dirt, or dust. But spiritual soap is available to reinvigorate and increase one's love for God. . .like coffee helps humans wake up and come alive on earth. (There is spiritual coffee in Heaven, and it is amazing…but that's a topic for another day.)

5. The day's schedule is flashed through each person's mind. The instant spontaneous reaction is to praise God and honor Him. We thrill at His Majesty and wisdom and are craving to experience more of God. There is so much more! An eternity awaits us.

"You have made known to me the path of life; you will fill me with joy in your presence, with eternal pleasures at your right hand." (Psalm 16:11)

"However, as it is written: No eye has seen, no ear has heard, no mind has conceived what God has prepared for those who love him' "] (1 Corinthians 2:9)

"Surely goodness and love will follow me all the days of my life, and I will dwell in the house of the Lord forever." (Psalm 23:6)

"Heaven is my throne and earth is my footstool." (Isaiah 66:1)

What if God treated us just like we treat Him?

The Scripture says that we should "do unto others as we would have them do to you." What if God treated us in Heaven the same way that we treat Him on earth? If that were the case, then those who love God more on earth would experience more of God's love in Heaven.

Those who are distant from God on earth, would experience distance from God in Heaven. All Christians will be in awesome Heaven. However lukewarm Christians may not comprehend the beauty and intimacy with God as vividly as those who have loved God more. Those who reject God on earth will be rejected by God and not allowed entrance into heaven.

Does God do unto us as we do unto Him? The answer to this is simple. "NO". If God treated us like we treat Him, He would cease to be God! He is Almighty God, and we should be so thankful that God does not and will not treat us like we treat Him.

"So in everything, do to others what you would have them do to you, for this sums up the Law and the Prophets." (Matthew 7:12)

"Jesus replied, 'Love the Lord your God with all your heart and with all your soul and with all your mind." (Matthew 22:37)

"For my thoughts are not your thoughts, neither are your ways my ways" declares the Lord. "As the Heavens are higher than the earth, so are my ways higher than your ways and my thoughts than your thoughts." (Isaiah 55:8,9)

"He does not treat us as our sins deserve or repay us according to our iniquities. For as high as the heavens are above the earth, so great is his love for those who fear Him;" But from everlasting to everlasting the Lord's love is with those who fear him. . ." (Psalm 103:10,11...17)

"Praise be to the God and Father or our Lord Jesus Christ, who has blessed us in the heavenly realms with every spiritual blessing in Christ." (Ephesians 1:3)

What if, after we die, we try to get to Heaven but get lost trying to find the place?

Where is Heaven and how do you find Heaven in all of creation? There is very good news for those who worry about getting lost easily. Christians will have no trouble finding Heaven. We will be in the best of company because Jesus knows the way and takes us there after we die!

"Do not let your hearts be troubled. Trust in God; trust also in me. In my Father's house are many rooms; if it were not so, I would have told you. I am going there to prepare a place for you. And if I go and prepare a place for you, I will come back and take you to be with me that you also may be where I am. (John 14:1-3)

"The Lord will guide you always. . ." (Isaiah 58:11)

"I am the Way, the Truth, and the Life. No man comes to the Father but through me." (John 14:6)

"When the perishable has been clothed with the imperishable and the mortal with immortality, then the saying that is written will come true; 'Death has been swallowed up in victory.'" (1 Corinthians 15:54)

"Even though I walk through the valley of the shadow of death, I will fear no evil, for you are with me; your rod and your staff they comfort me. Surely goodness and love will follow me all the days of my life, and I will dwell in the house of the Lord forever." (Psalm 24:4,6)

What if you have decided to end it all and the time is now?

You are topped off with depression; there is no hope. This is the moment! There is no reason to keep on. The pills or trigger or bridge have been decided upon. The time is now. You take a deep breath and look around one last time.

Heart pounding, head throbbing, you feel excitement with fear about what the next world will be like. Another second passes and then another. You take another big, deep breath.

Why not wait just one more hour before ending life? Why not experience Mom or a loved one just one more time? Could there be a breakthrough in medicine discovered tomorrow that would make a difference? Why let someone else use my money and car? Would I miss out on even a little love or laughter in the future? Would I miss out on something really good if I pull the trigger? (John 10:10)---DON'T MISS IT!

"I have come that they may have life, and have it to the full." (John 10:10b)

". . .Now choose life, so that you and your children may live and that you may love the Lord your God, listen to his voice, and hold fast to him. For the Lord is your life, and he will give you many years in the land. . ." (Deuteronomy 30:19, 20)

"Be strong and courageous. Do not be terrified; do not be discouraged, for the Lord your God will be with you wherever you go." (Joshua 1:9)

"Even though I walk through the valley of the shadow of death, I will fear no evil, for you are with me; your rod and your staff they comfort me." (Psalm 23:4)

What if God seriously rewards good behavior?

It is true that we can't 'manipulate' God, nor force Him to do something because of our specific actions. On the other hand, there seems to be a very strong relationship between His blessing us when we do what He desires us to do. The opposite is true as well. He disciplines those He loves when they deliberately disobey.

The positive/negative reward system is so simple and universal. It is how we train our children and pets. It's how we achieve our best in school. It is why we prefer to be good and not bad. It makes leaders and discourages criminals.

Does God also use the positive/negative reward system? O course! It is His system and it works. It is a wonderful method that God uses to bless each of us and also to keep us out of trouble. Enjoy God's "positive reward" system and utilize it as much as possible. God promises to bless you through your good behavior. The blessing may not be immediate or exactly what you expected, but sooner or later you will experience God's blessing because of your faithfulness and obedience.

"Do not let this Book of the Law depart from your mouth; meditate on it day and night, so that you may be careful to do everything written in it. Then you will be prosperous and successful." (Joshua 1:8)

"Therefore, take care to follow the commands, decrees, and laws I give you today. If you pay attention to these laws and are careful to follow them, then the Lord your God will keep his covenant of love with you...He will love you and bless you and increase your numbers. He will bless the fruit of your womb, the crops of your land. . ." (Deuteronomy 7: 11-13)

"The Lord will make you the head, not the tail, if you pay attention to the commands of the Lord your God that I give you this day and carefully follow them, you will always be at the top, never at the bottom. (Deuteronomy 28:13)

"Delight yourself in the Lord and He will give you the desires of your heart." (Psalm 37:4)

What if Jesus invited you to spend five minutes helping Him anytime during His earthly life?

Which five minutes would you choose to help? Would you help distribute bread and fish to 5,000 people? Would you want to help with crowd control when Lazarus rose from the dead? Or would you help protect Jesus when He overturned the tax collectors tables? That would be exciting and helpful. The options are so many!

It seems clear, however, that Jesus wanted help most intensely in the Garden of Gethsemane. He was deep in prayer, sweating drops of blood. It was there that He earnestly asked his disciples to pray for Him. That may have been the one time in his life when He desperately asked for personal help. He strongly desired others to pray for Him.

Is it too late to pray for Christ 2,000 years later and still have our prayers added to those of the sleepy disciples? In some wonderful way, God knows our thoughts, and He is beyond time. He is the beginning and the end all at the same time. Perhaps He can take our prayers for Him that we pray today and benefit from them back in time at Gethsemane. Our five minutes of love and prayer for Jesus today may still be felt by Jesus in His greatest moment of need.

Vicariously join with the disciples on that intense night, and pray five minutes earnestly for the Lord. (Don't fall asleep!)

"For nothing is impossible with God." (Luke 1:37)

"I am the Alpha and the Omega, the First and the Last, the Beginning and the End." (Revelation 22:13)

"I have been crucified with Christ and I no longer live, but Christ lives in me. The life I live in the body, I live by faith in the Son of God, who loved me and gave himself for me." (Galatians 2:20)

"For from him and through him and to him are all things. To him be glory for ever. Amen" (Romans 11:36)

"For a thousand years in your sight are like a day that has just gone by, or like a watch in the night." (Psalm 90:4)

What if you could monitor Jesus' thoughts during the beginning of His 40-day fast in the wilderness?

What would He be thinking about, and what Scripture would He use to answer his thoughts? : "Jesus, full of the Holy Spirit, returned from the Jordan and was led by the Spirit in the desert, where for forty days he was tempted by the devil. He ate nothing during those days and at the end of them he was hungry." (Luke 4:1,2)

The following are speculations regarding what Jesus might have written down if He had a prayer journal.

"Thank you Father for the nights rest and for waking me up so early. The sunrise is very, very nice.   I remember the joy We experienced creating sunrise possibilities with beautiful colors and spectacular rays of light."

"In the beginning was the Word (Jesus), and the Word was with God, and the Word was God. He was with God in the beginning. Through him all things were made; without him nothing was made that has been made" (John 1:1-3)

<u>"Father, I want to accomplish your will today."</u>
"Our Father in heaven, hallowed be your name, your kingdom come, your will be done on earth as it is in heaven." (Matthew 6:9, 10)

"For I have come down from heaven not to do my will but to do the will of him who sent me." (John 6:38)

<u>"Why are the ants and spiders and flies that I made biting me?"</u>
"For we do not have a high priest who is unable to sympathize with our weaknesses, but we have one who has been tempted in every way, just as we are--yet was without sin." (Hebrews 4:15)

"Let everything that has breath praise the Lord. Praise the Lord." (Psalm 150:6)

<u>'Thank you Holy Spirit for providing for all my needs in this wilderness. By your power and strength I will accomplish the Father's will today.'</u>
"I can do everything through him who gives me strength." (Philippians 4:13)
"And my God will meet all your needs according to his glorious riches in Christ Jesus." (Philippians 4:19)

<u>I love You, Father.</u>

"Our Father in heaven, hallowed be your name, your kingdom come, your will be done on earth as it is in heaven." (Matthew 6:9, 10)"

"Jesus replied: 'Love the Lord your God with all your heart and with all your soul and with all your mind.'" (Matthew 23:37)

What if you could monitor Jesus' life near the end of his 40-day fast in the wilderness?

He knows that Satan will be tempting Him three times on Day 40? What would He be thinking about and praying about?

The following might be a sample from His "diary of thoughts" and the Scripture that He used on the morning of Day 37:

<u>"I'm getting hungry. Thank you that your Word is bread to me."</u>
Taste and see that the Lord is good; blessed is the man who takes refuge in him." (Psalm 34:8) "The lions may grow weak and hungry, but those who seek the Lord lack no good thing." (Psalm 34:10)

"How sweet are your words to my taste, sweeter than honey to my mouth! (Psalm 119:103)

Jesus answered, "It is written" 'Man does not live on bread alone, but on every word that comes from the mouth of God." (Matthew 4:4)

"I resist you Satan. Flee!"

"Submit yourselves, then, to God. Resist the devil, and he will flee from you. Come near to God and he will come near to you." (James 4:7,8)

"I want to be with You, Father."

"As the deer pants for streams of water, so my soul pants for you, O God. My soul thirsts for God, for the living God." (Psalm 42:1,2)

"Your will be done. I trust in You."

"Father I have come down from heaven not to do my will but to do the will of him who sent me." (John 6:38)

"Trust in the Lord with all your heart and lean not on your own understanding; in all your ways acknowledge him, and he will make your paths straight." (Proverbs 3:5, 60)

"Be joyful always; pray continually; give thanks in all circumstances, for this is God's will for you in Christ Jesus." (1 Thessalonians 5:16-18)

"I have nothing more to say."

"Be still and know that I am God." (Psalm 46:10)

What if the "default position" sends most people to Hell?

Each person during their lifetime has the wonderful opportunity to choose to go to Heaven instead of Hell. Circumstances and opportunities for "choice exposure" vary from one individual to another but, when it's all over, each person independently chooses one eternal fate or the other. Unfortunately many well meaning people never get around to making the decision. It is not that they have chosen not to become Christians. They simply haven't made the decision yet. What happens to them?

Indecision is not a safe place to be in. Many people chose to live in indecision their entire lives. This results in many people slipping into Hell by default. That is, many slip into Hell because they didn't get around to making a choice for Heaven.

 "Now fear the LORD and serve him with all faithfulness. Throw away the gods your forefathers worshiped beyond the River and in Egypt, and serve the Lord. But if serving the LORD seems undesirable to you, then choose for yourselves this day whom you will serve, whether the gods your forefathers served beyond the River, or the gods of the Amorites, in whose land you are living. But as for me and my household, we will serve the LORD." (Joshua 24:1415)

I tell you, now is the time of God's favor, now is the day of salvation. (2 Corinthians 6:2)

"He who **is** not with **me is against me**, and he who does not gather with **me** scatters. (Matthew 12:30)

"Enter through the narrow gate. For wide is the gate and broad is the road that leads to destruction, and many enter through it. But small is the gate and narrow the road that leads to life, and only a few find it." (Matthew 7:13, 14)

What if life on earth is just a simple battle between God and Satan?

It's the old thrilling "good versus evil" theme that runs constantly through many novels, movies and TV shows. God on one side is very loving, all powerful, and can destroy Satan easily. However, God limits his power severely. He will not over power the free will among the combatants.

The clock on earth's battle field has been wound up and is now steadily ticking down. At some point, known only to God, the battle will be victoriously won by God. He is definitely in control. It is as though "The battle is won, but not yet!"

The combatants' task on earth is to find God as quickly as possible in their lives. Then obey Him and do whatever He says in order to fight Satan. To do this the combatants will be given armor, weapons, supernatural guidance (on where and how to fight) and unlimited power from God if they ask for it.

The only rule for the battle is that combatants have total "Free Will". God will not force combatants to choose to be on His side. Each combatant must choose whether they want to fight on God's side with His power or on Satan's side with Satan's power. Combatants may hide from the battle which ends in the default position.

"Choose for yourselves this day whom you will serve...But as for me and my household, we will serve the Lord." (Joshua 24:15)

"Do not be afraid of them; the Lord your God himself will fight for you." (Deuteronomy 3:22)

"Be strong and courageous. Do not be terrified; do not be discouraged, for the Lord your God will be with you wherever you go." (Joshua 1:9)

"...what does the Lord your God ask of you but to fear the Lord your God, to walk in all his ways, to love him, to serve the Lord your God with all your heart and with all your soul, and to observe the Lord's command and decrees that I am giving you today for your own good?" (Deuteronomy 10:12, 13)

"For the Lord your God is the one who goes with you to fight for you against your enemies to give you victory." (Deuteronomy 20:4)

"This is what the Lord says to you: 'Do not be afraid or discouraged because of this vast army. For the battle is not your, but God's." (2 Chronicles 19:15)

"Praise be to the Lord, my Rock, who trains my hands for war, my fingers for battle." (Psalm 144:1)

"If you make the Most High your dwelling-even the Lord, who is my refuge-then no harm will befall you, no disaster will come near your tent." "Because he loves me," says the Lord, "I will protect him, for he acknowledges my name. He will call upon me, and I will answer him. I will be with him in trouble. I will deliver him and honor him. With long life will I satisfy him and show him my salvation." (Psalm 91:9, 14-16)

"Finally, be strong in the Lord and in his mighty power. Put on the full armor of God so that you can take your stand against the devil's schemes. For our struggle is not against flesh and blood, but against the rulers, against the authorities, against the power of this dark world and against the spiritual forces of evil in the heavenly realms.

Therefore put on the full armor of God, so that when the day of evil comes, you may be able to stand your ground, and after you have done everything, to stand. Stand firm them, with the belt of truth bucked around your waist, with the breastplate of righteousness in place, and with your feet fitted with the readiness that comes from the gospel of peace.

In addition to all this, take up the shield of faith, with which you can extinguish all the flaming arrows of the evil one. Take the helmet of salvation and the sword of the Spirit which is the word of God. And pray in the Spirit on all occasions with all kinds of prayers and requests." (Ephesians 6:10-18)

What if someone died and went to the gates of Heaven and the doorkeeper asked the person; "Why should I let you into Heaven?"

He or she said; "Because I'm a pretty good person. I'm more good than bad and I deserve to enter Heaven."

Another said; "My parents are Christian and I go to church sometimes."

Another said; "I act like a Christian and I'm not as bad as some Christian hypocrites."

Another said; "I feel godly when I'm out in nature and I think that there is a god who possibly made all of this."

Another said; "By God's Grace, because of my faith in Jesus Christ who died for my sins and is Lord of my life."

"WELL DONE GOOD AND FAITHFUL SERVANT. ENTER INTO GOD'S HEAVEN MADE FOR YOU!"

"That if you confess with your mouth, 'Jesus is Lord,' and believe in your heart that God raised him from the dead, you will be saved." (Romans 10:9)

"Jesus answered, 'I am the way and the truth and the life. No one comes to the Father except through me." (John 14:6)

"Yet to all who received him, to those who believed in his name, he gave the right to become children of God." (John 14:6)

"For it is by grace you have been saved, through faith—and this not from yourselves, it is the gift of God—not by works, so that no one can boast." (Ephesians 2:8, 9)

What if God were to reveal the most spectacular activity in all of creation to us?

What would that activity be? In Ezekiel and Revelation, God describes His Throne Room! What occurs there probably is the most significant activity in the entire universe.

In His Throne Room God reveals an ever-increasing revelation of Himself and His Glory for all Christians to see. For all eternity saints will experience more and more of God's "spectacular awesomeness" as great time periods pass. These ever increasing revelations will result in our praising God because of the immense thrill from the revelations. The following six worship words will be continually on our lips in response to God's awesomeness: "PRAISE AND HONOR, GLORY AND MAJESTY, WISDOM AND POWER!"

We will delight to praise and boast about God Himself due to ever increasing revelations. There will not be prayer requests or confessions of wrongdoings. These don't occur in the Throne Room. Rather, there will be wonderful adoration in the forms of worship and praise because God is so awesome beyond our utmost imagination.

Praise and worship will be the most significant activity in all of creation because God is the main event and absolutely nothing in all of creation comes even close to competing with God!

"Above the expanse over their heads was what looked like a throne of sapphire, and high above on the throne was a figure like that of a man. I saw that from what appeared to be his waist up he looked like glowing metal, as if full of fire, and then from there down he looked like fire; a brilliant light surrounded him. Like the appearance of a rainbow in the clouds on a rainy day, so was the radiance around Him. This was the appearance of the likeness of the glory of the Lord. When I saw it, I fell facedown, and I heard the voice of one speaking." (Ezekiel 1:26-28)

"In a loud voice they sang: 'Worthy is the Lamb, who was slain, to receive power and wealth and wisdom and strength and honor and glory and praise!'" (Revelation 5:12)

"You are worthy, our Lord and God, to receive glory and honor and power, for you created all things, and by your will they were created and have their being." (Revelation 4:11)

"Father, I (Jesus) want those you have given me to be with me where I am, and to see my glory, the glory you have given me because you loved me before the creation of the world." (John 17:24)

What if you actually are plural?

Christians, in a miraculous way, are plural! Once a person becomes a Christian, they change from being solo to being plural. Let me explain. Initially at conception, God has placed a spirit within the living embryo which is made in the "image of God". At some later point, the person may choose to become a Christian. That is when a very important change occurs and the person becomes a "new creation". At this conversion the Holy Spirit enters into the person and he or she becomes plural; one spirit joined by the Holy Spirit!

The person's spirit will always be in charge of the major executive decisions and can overrule the Holy Spirit's suggestions. On the other hand, the person may at any time invite the Holy Spirit to help more and even take control. This is very helpful because the Holy Spirit is able to make improvements that would be impossible without supernatural help.

The Holy Spirit within a person is particularly helpful in the following activities: (this list is small but the actual list is infinite!)

- Guiding service. (Isaiah 58:11)
- Housecleaning service. (Philippians 2:12, 13)
- Intelligence boosting service. (James 1:5)
- Anger, depression, fear counseling service. (John 14:16, 17)

- Retirement planning service. (2 Corinthians 1:22)

So many people live their lives being lonely. To become plural is a wonderful opportunity to gain a "live in" friend who affords benefits beyond our imagination and should never to be taken lightly!

"Therefore, if anyone is in Christ, he is a new creation; the old has gone, the new has come!" (2 Corinthians 5:17) "Do you not know that your body is a temple of the Holy Spirit who is in you, whom you have received from God?" (1 Corinthians 6:19)

"I will guide you always." (Isaiah 58:11) "But when He, the Sprit of Truth, comes He will guide you into all truth." (John 16:13)

"Continue to work out your salvation with fear and trembling, for it is God Who works in you to will and to act according to His good purpose." (Philippians 2:12, 13)

"If any of you lacks wisdom, he should ask God, Who gives generously to all without finding fault, and it will be given to him." (James 1:5)

"And I will ask the Father, and He will give you another Counselor to be with you forever—the Sprit of Truth...for He lives with you and will be in you." (John 14:16, 17)

"He (God) anointed us, set His seal of ownership on us, and put His Spirit in our hearts as a deposit, guaranteeing what is to come." (2 Corinthians 1:22)

What if you were to receive a deposit of remarkable value?

Each of us, when we become a Christian, receive a "Deposit of the Holy Spirit". The Holy Spirit miraculously joins with our spirit in a supernatural manner. When we die, the Holy Spirit, joined with our spirit, go together into Heaven. The Holy Spirit living within us is our guarantee that Heaven will be our destination. (It would be impossible for the Holy Spirit to be sent to Hell.)

The Holy Spirit deposit is only available for Christians and is given at the time of salvation. The deposit is free and can be obtained at any age, often during the teenage years but may be as early as 3 years of age. The Holy Spirit provides faith, love and power to Christians if asked to do so. Unfortunately, many Christians fail to invite the Holy Spirit to empower them and as a result struggle through life using only their own strength. If you are a Christian, pray that the Holy Spirit will unleash His power in your life.

"Now it is God Who makes both us and you stand firm in Christ. He anointed us, set his seal of ownership on us, and put his Spirit in our hearts as a deposit guaranteeing what is to come." (2 Corinthians 1:21, 22)

"Having believed, you were marked in him with a seal, the promised Holy Spirit, who is a deposit guaranteeing our inheritance until the redemption of those who are God's possession –to the praise of his Glory." (Ephesians 1:13, 14)

"But you will receive power when the Holy Spirit comes on you; and you will be my witnesses in Jerusalem...and to the ends of the earth." (Acts1:8)

"I keep asking that God... may give you the Spirit of Wisdom and Revelation (Holy Spirit) so that you may know...his incomparably great power for us who believe. That power is like the working of his mighty strength, which he exerted in Christ when he raised him from the dead and seated him at his right hand in the heavenly realms..." (Ephesians 1:17, 19)

What if Christians have a wonderful inheritance promised to each of them and the inheritance provisions can be known today?

The inheritance is spectacular, providing for beautiful mansion-like accommodations, wealth, great health, and special loved ones. These wonderful provisions make planning the rest of one's life much easier. The provisions may free you up to risk your wealth and talents now in more Godly ways than you normally would. Focusing major energy toward loving God and loving others would make sense rather than spending a lifetime accumulating wealth and possessions which would be so small compared to your upcoming inheritance.

Risk big time for the Lord now with what you have. Your future needs will be provided for quite well with your inheritance.

"Yet to all who received him (Jesus), to those who believed in his name, he gave the right to become children of God." (John 1:12)

"Surely goodness and love will follow me all the days of my life and I will dwell in the House of the Lord forever." (Psalm 23:6) "In my Father's house are many rooms...I am going there to prepare a place for you...that you may also be where I am." (John 14:2,3)

"Then the King (Jesus) will say to those on his right, 'Come, you who are blessed by my Father; take your inheritance, the Kingdom prepared for you since the creation of the world. For I was hungry and you gave me something to eat, I was thirsty and you gave me something to drink, I was a stranger and you invited me in, I needed clothes and you clothed me, I was sick and you looked after me, I was in prison and you came to visit me...I tell you the truth, whatever you did for one of the least of these brothers of mine, you did for me." (Matthew 25:34-36, 40)

"And everyone who has left houses or brothers or sisters or father or mother or children or fields for my sake will receive a hundred times as much and will inherit eternal life." (Matthew 19:29)

"Having believed, you were marked in him with a seal, the promised Holy Spirit, who is a deposit guaranteeing our inheritance until the redemption of those who are God's possession –to the praise of his Glory." (Ephesians 1:13, 14)

"He ...showed me the Holy City, Jerusalem, coming down out of heaven from God. It shone with the glory of God and its brilliance was like that of a very precious jewel, like a jasper, clear as crystal... The wall was made of jasper, and the city of pure gold as pure as glass... The great street of the city was of pure gold, like transparent glass." (Revelation 21:10, 11, 18, 21)

"Praise be to the God and Father of our Lord Jesus Christ, who has blessed us in the heavenly realms with every spiritual blessing in Christ." (Ephesians 1:3)

Dr. Henry Jacob Rupp is a physician living in St. Paul Minnesota. He and Sandy, his wife and 4 children were missionaries in East Africa for 15 years serving with Africa Inland Mission and Mission: Moving Mountains. He attended Bethel Seminary, St. Paul, Minnesota during furlough years. His passion is to grow closer to the Lord and enjoy Him forever.

"What If" has been written at "the Shack" while sitting in a lazy boy recliner on Monday mornings watching God's wonderful creation from the front room window.

 In addition to his medical work, Dr. Rupp is an oil painting instructor and amateur taxidermist.

++++++++++++++++++++++++++++++++++++
All profit from this book beyond printing/ postage costs are sent directly into foreign missions.

Contact jaysandyrupp@q.com to order additional books ($10/book-$1Postage) or send a check to: "What If"
                        3472 North Milton Street
                        St. Paul, Minnesota, 55126.